APOLOGY FOR WONDER

SAM KEEN

APOLOGY FOR WONDER

1817

Harper & Row, Publishers

New York, Evanston, and London

LIBRARY OF CONGRESS CATALOG CARD NUMBER: 69–17017

ACKNOWLEDGMENTS

Epigram from *The Martian Chronicles* by Ray Bradbury reprinted by permission of Doubleday & Company, Inc.

Lines from *Winnie-the-Pooh* by A. A. Milne copyright 1926 by E. P. Dutton & Co., Inc., renewal 1954 by A. A. Milne. Reprinted by permission of the publishers.

Lines from "The Love Song of J. Alfred Prufrock" by T. S. Eliot, from *Collected Poems 1909–1962,* reprinted by permission of Harcourt, Brace & World, Inc.

Lines from Epictetus in A. I. Melden, ed., *Ethical Theories: A Book of Readings,* 2nd edition, © 1955 Prentice-Hall, Inc., Englewood Cliffs, N. J. Reprinted by permission.

Chart from *Book of the Hopi* by Frank Waters, Drawings and source material recorded by Oswald White Bear Fredericks, copyright © 1963 by Frank Waters. All rights reserved. Reprinted by permission of The Viking Press, Inc.

FOR MY FATHER

J. ALVIN KEEN (1899–1964)

And how can I say why?

His life was anchored in the great simplicities of earth:
The touch of the lithe bodies of children,
The hue of polished stones,
The astringent sun and antiseptic air of the desert,
The elegant geometry of shells and driftwood long bathed in the sea,
The perfume of early blooming lilacs,
The silent testimony of redwood trees,
The refreshment of all that is beautiful and graceful.

And yet there was the resonance of those elusive harmonies at which
    music hints and for which faith strives.
He lived with a growing ability
To deepen the covenants of friendship,
To admire simplicity and dedication,
To accept limitations and disappointments without resentment,
To forgive the unacceptable and trust the unknown,
To love without grasping,
To be grateful for the gift of life.

In his ambience I learned that it is a good thing to take time to
    wonder.

7

CONTENTS

If there be a skeptical star I was born under it,
Yet I have lived all my days in complete astonishment.
                              —W. MacNeile Dixon[1]

This is a book about wonder. It is about many other things as
well: traditional and modern models of man, changing modes of
experiencing and expressing the holy, and the nature of authentic
life. Now that I have finished writing and must tell you how to
begin reading, I can do no better than resort to a slightly grandiose
fantasy I had as I neared the end of my task.

One day, as my eyes delighted in the sight of a tall pile of neatly
typed manuscript pages and my idling mind wandered, I imagined
a photographer appearing at the door of my office with the task
assigned of taking a picture of me for the dust jacket of this book.
When I learned his purpose, I began to question myself: "What
is the appropriate background for such a photograph? Where, symbolically, was I standing as I wrote about wonder?"

Unfortunately, my imaginary photographer, anxious to finish in
time for a luncheon date, did not share my passion for symbolic
backgrounds. Seeing a bone-white wall outside my office, he suggested that such a neutral background would be ideal. Something
in me rebelled! A philosopher does not work against a neutral
background. It is useless to try to hide the autobiographical
foundations of philosophy—to pretend that the diagnoses and

13

prescriptions offered concerning the human condition emerge from an off-white, neutral analysis of anonymous facts. No, philosophy arises out of the spiritual need to clarify what we may responsibly believe and feel and how we must act if we are to be profoundly, rather than superficially, human. All philosophy begins in autobiography. If it is anything more than a crossword puzzle designed to stun our awareness of the bittersweet transience of life, philosophy is a search for the universal in the particular and the eternal in the fleeting. Since I began exploring wonder with the hope of understanding Sam Keen, I had to reject the suggestion of an antiseptic background as symbolically appropriate.

My photographer next suggested that the shelves of books that line my office might form a good traditional background. Without question, most books written by professors are a series of conversations with other authors and significant colleagues. In these pages the reader will easily detect a running dialogue with Tom Altizer, Hannah Arendt, Norman Brown, Albert Camus, G. K. Chesterton, Nikos Kazantzakis, D. H. Lawrence, Gabriel Marcel, Jean Paul Sartre, Paul Tillich, and a host of other writers. Yet, I have learned more of wonder from flesh than from paper: from talk that comes only when friends eat together—from Ted Brown, Tom Green, Jim Gagnon, Jane Everett, Howard Thurman, Manny and Sylvia Maier, Dick Ruopp, Dave Scott, and many others with whom I have shared wine and ideas; from my wife, Heather, who taught me to dance; from my children, who are teaching me to take time for their world; from my parents, who taught me things I am just beginning to understand; from a fleeting glimpse I caught, one February afternoon in Harvard Square, of a brown face and red lips; and, once, from three sterling silver notes a wood thrush sang against a dark green twilight. The school in which I learned to wonder is filled more with persons, places, and things than with books.

By now, reconciled to missing his luncheon date, my imaginary photographer began to warm to the task of discovering the proper symbolic setting. As we walked from the office out into the open air, we came to the modern-Gothic chapel, with the phallic campanile rising by its side, that occupies a prominent position on campus. Certainly this place would provide just the right flavor of the holy and the erotic! To wonder is to perceive with reverence and love (*eros*), and in wondering we come close to the feeling that the earth is holy. Historically, the notion of wonder has been closely bound up with a religious mode of being in the world. Perhaps a century ago the chapel would have been an appropriate background, but now things seem to have changed. The sanctuary is so seldom filled with vitality and enthusiasm. The words are still there: "celebration," "joy," "hope," "love." But the music drags, and there is no dancing and little radical openness to surprise and change. In my experience, the substance of wonder is more frequently found in the prose of the secular than in the often quaint poetry of religion. The sacred is in the profane; the holy is in the quotidian; the wonder is in the world.

Walking down the hill from the chapel into the park, we came to a spot called Big Rock, where Beargrass Creek runs by some sizable cliffs and boulders. As my eye fell upon an island of sand, cast up by the current between the rock and the stream, some voice within me gave its consent. Here was the place—between the running water and the rock, the flux and the abiding, the skeptical star and the amazement.

Man has always known of time and the river. Neither Heraclitus nor Thomas Wolfe invented the tragic knowledge that we can never step twice in the same place in the stream of time or return to the innocence that was our home before we became aware of transitoriness. But for many modern men the current has become swift and terrifying, because the conviction has been lost that the river flows either from or into any oceanic reservoir of meaning. The river has become a flood tide, washing away past certainties and undermining the metaphysical foundations of identity. Relativism and nihilism are solvents of identity which threaten all who live where the intellectual currents of the twentieth century converge.

Although, like most modern men, I have had to struggle against despair in the polluted waters of nihilism, from time to time my feet have found the rock. In spite of the skeptical star, I have never ceased to live in amazement. This book is an effort to examine the rock and the river—wonder and skepticism. The questions I asked myself in the process of this investigation will serve as the best introduction to the intent of the individual chapters of this book.

1. What does it mean to wonder? The opening chapter takes the experience of wonder apart and examines its components. This descriptive, or phenomenological, analysis prepares the way for broader speculation about the significance of wonder for authentic human life.

2. Why do we associate wonder with childhood? Chapter II isolates some of the characteristics of childish thought and experience which allow wonder to be the native atmosphere of healthy childhood.

3. What part did wonder play in the self-understanding of pre-modern man? Is it mere romanticism to suppose that technological knowledge has led to an eclipse of a sense of wonder that was the common property of traditional man? The third chapter deals with three traditional world views (archaic, Greek, and Judeo-Christian), all of which envisage man as *homo admirans* and thus assign wonder a prominent place in the attitudes which are essential for authentic human life.

4. How did the skeptical star arise which signaled the end of amazement for so many who call themselves "modern men"? What is the place of wonder in the world view and self-understanding that is coming to characterize technological society? Chapter IV deals with the changing spiritual ecology in which modern man is nurtured, the emerging consensus concerning the absurdity or carelessness of all nonhuman reality. Chapter V traces the logic of what is, perhaps, the most representative contemporary model of man—*homo faber*.

5. How should wonder function within the economy of the healthy personality? Assuming that neither the naïveté of the traditional notion of man as *homo admirans* nor the spiritual poverty of the model of man as *homo faber* is any longer acceptable, for reasons I hope are made clear, the sixth chapter of this book suggests some principles for construction of a more adequate model of man, or a theory of maturity.

6. Does wonder inevitably lead to worship and the development of a theological rhetoric? A final chapter explores both

secular and religious expressions of the grace and gratitude that spring from a wondering intuition of the world.

One further word is necessary to identify the discipline within which the type of reflection carried on in this book is located. Although philosophy begins in autobiography, it does not end there. A philosopher must search in the concrete for the universal; he must discover where the personal and the idiosyncratic join the communal—where the private meets the public. While this book was born out of a quest for self-understanding, it seeks to demonstrate that the attitude of wonder it explores is a prerequisite of authentic humanness. This demonstration is at once a presentation and a defense of wonder. It is for this reason that the archaic word "apology" appears in the title. An apology was originally understood as a defense a man made before a court—for instance, Socrates' defense of his life and philosophy before the Athenian court. In the second century of the Christian era a number of philosopher-theologians appeared who are commonly referred to as apologists. These men stood with one foot in the Christian (or Jewish) community and one foot in the philosophical world of their day and tried to discover the common ground shared by all thinking men. They found in the notion of *logos* (word-reason) the assumption shared by all men of good will: all men, they believed, had an innate confidence in the reasonable character of reality. This idealistic faith in the rationality of the real (and vice versa) has evaporated in our time. Hence, contemporary philosophers and theologians must enter into conversation again to search for that principle which is the guarantor of the sanctity of human life. This book is an offering and an invitation to such a conversation. It rests upon the conviction that such basic attitudes as wonder, hope, and trust provide us with universals which are essential to vivid human life. If man is to survive as man, he must never cease wondering.

A word on how to read this book may be helpful. The method followed here is inductive. The book begins with phenomenological and historical analysis and proceeds only gradually to conclusions. Thus in both content and style the sections having the most immediate existential payoff are in the final chapters. Too much "religious" writing begins with conclusions, pronouncements, and recommendations. At the risk of demanding a long attention span of its reader, an apology proceeds to speculation only after establishing an empirical foundation; it dances only after analysis. I am aware that I might have caught your attention more rapidly by beginning at the end. I hope, however, that you will labor with me through the analysis in the heat of the day, so that when we come to dance in the evening our feet may be firmly grounded. But if you are the type who reads the end of a mystery novel first, or if long reading of theology has accustomed you to having conclusions before investigations, you may turn first to Chapter VI, p. 190, "Wonder and Authentic Life." (I send with this invitation a mild slap on the wrist to the three out of four readers who will not be able to resist it.)

Finally, I would like to express my gratitude to many friends, colleagues, and students who have helped to make this a better book than it would have been without their critiques and suggestions (especially Bob Brown, Joe McCown, David Steere, Alan Schneider, and Guy Wilcox, who read and commented upon portions of this manuscript). I am also grateful to Louisville Presbyterian Seminary for the freedom from pressure that has made writing possible, and to my typist, Elaine David, for much help in matters grammatical and for loving attention to detail.

APOLOGY FOR WONDER

Wonder is based upon the feeling that at the deepest levels the world and man's true self are one. This means that the aspirations and ideals, the beauty and goodness, which are natural to the human heart, lie somehow also at the center of the physical universe; that therefore standards of beauty and goodness are not irrelevant to the realities of an indifferent world, but are quite as pertinent to the study of universal events as are the quantitative standards of physical science.

JOHN GARDNER[1]

CHAPTER I

The Anatomy
of Wonder

What does it mean to wonder? We have all had experiences in which elements of the uncanny, the wonderful, the awful, and the holy are vaguely mixed. Most often the outlines of wonder are not sufficiently distinct to allow us to identify its essence and distinguish it from its close relatives. By outlining the anatomy or phenomenology of wonder we may see how it is like and unlike awe, curiosity, reverence, and other related experiences. This will prepare us to investigate the significance of wonder in traditional and modern models of man and to judge whether it must be present in any fully authentic life.

A study in anatomy begins most easily with a healthy specimen. Therefore our phenomenology of wonder will proceed by analyzing the mature experience of wonder. In speaking of a mature, healthy, or authentic sense of wonder we are obviously making use of terms that are normative and not merely descriptive. Were we to describe wonder as it exists in the experience of the average person in our culture, we might well have to conclude that there is no such phenomenon. The justification for introducing a normative perspective will emerge from the total analysis and argument of this book.

Our method will be (1) to deal with the types and characteristics of the objects of wonder, then (2) to focus on the subjective aspects of the experience, and finally (3) to compare wonder to its nearest relative—the experience of the holy.

1. THE OBJECTS OF WONDER

ONTOLOGIC WONDER

What kinds of objects and events trigger the sense of wonder?

The primal source of all wonder is not an object but the fact that something exists rather than nothing. With considerable shock the mind is sometimes jarred into the realization that there is no necessary reason for the existence of the world or anything in it. As Wittgenstein has said, "It is not *how* things are in the world that is mystical, but *that* it exists."[2] In speaking of the same matter, Tillich said that, viewed from the standpoint of the possibility of nonbeing, being is a mystery. However odd it may be linguistically or logically, there are states of mind in which the very existence of the world seems strange and miraculous, as if its being were a triumph over nothingness.

It is this primal or ontologic wonder that philosophers have traditionally thought of as the wellspring of man's quest for an explanation of his place under the sun. When the brute givenness of reality is experienced in wonder, certainties give way to questions which, so long as wonder remains, can never receive final answers. William James has commented on this insatiable character of wonder.

Existence then will be a brute fact to which as a whole the emotion of ontologic wonder shall rightfully cleave, but remain eternally unsatisfied. Then wonderfulness or mysteriousness will be an essential attribute of the nature of things, and the exhibition and emphasizing of it will continue to be an ingredient in the philosophic industry of the race.[3]

So long as explanations are elaborated in the light of the mystery of being, wonder remains a source and principle of philosophy, science, art, and religion.

MUNDANE WONDER

There is a second type of wonder which is elicited primarily by *what* a thing is rather than *that* it is. We may refer to this as mundane wonder. Most often wonder arises out of an encounter with some concrete object or person and not out of a global awareness of the mystery of being. In such encounters the structure and meaning of the object rather than its bare existence are the occasion for wonder. There could be no adequate catalogue of the objects that produce such mundane wonder: a loved person, a gnarled tree, a beautiful stone, a "miraculous" event, and so on.

The Sensational

Most frequently mundane wonder is evoked by encountering something novel and sensational. If we take common linguistic usage as a criterion, we might conclude that wonder had to do primarily with objects or events of a prodigious nature. We speak frequently of the "wonders of nature" or the "wonders of science." Ray Bradbury has prefaced his *Martian Chronicles* with the epigram:

> It is a good thing to renew our sense of wonder.
> Space travel has made children of us all again.

While this may be an overly optimistic estimate of what space travel has accomplished, it does point out the relation between the sensational and the experience of wonder. It is unfortunate but true that wonder is often experienced only on the frontier of the startling. The first astronaut encircling the globe was an occasion for wonder, but the subsequent ones were merely occasions for entertainment. Discoveries which a generation ago produced wonder at the ingenuity of man now elicit only a yawn. One may venture the prediction that the news of the second man to land on the moon will arouse some interest but little wonder. Wonder, at this point, will be in a state of suspended animation until the first man lands on Mars.

The Familiar

A mature sense of wonder does not need the constant titillation of the sensational to keep it alive. It is most often called forth by a confrontation with the mysterious depth of meaning at the heart of the familiar and quotidian. Rare birds—the scarlet tanagers and indigo buntings of experience—do upon occasion delight us, but a mature sense of wonder may be evoked by starlings and English sparrows. One is reminded of the incident in *Zorba the Greek* when Zorba and the boss meet a peasant riding on a donkey.

> One day, I remember, when we were making our way to the village, we met a little old man astride a mule. Zorba opened his eyes wide as he looked at the beast. And his look was so intense that the peasant cried out in terror:
> "For God's sake, brother, don't give him the evil eye!" And he crossed himself.
> I turned to Zorba.
> "What did you do to the old chap to make him cry out like that?" I asked him.
> "Me? What d' you think I did? I was looking at his mule, that's all! Didn't it strike you, boss?"
> "What?"
> "Well . . . that there are such things as mules in this world!"[4]

FORMAL CHARACTERISTICS OF THE OBJECTS OF WONDER

While many types of objects, sensational and ordinary, may evoke the sense of wonder, there are some formal characteristics common to all.

Contingency

The philosophical term "contingency" most accurately describes one characteristic of objects as they are given to us in wonder. As used here, contingency means that in raw experience the object we apprehend in wonder comes to us without bearing its own explanation. Why it is, or perhaps even what it is, is not immediately obvious. In less philosophical but more modern terminology, wonder-events are happenings, revelatory occurrences which appear, as if by chance, bearing some new meaning (value, promise) which cannot immediately be integrated into a past pattern of understanding and explanation.

Mystery

A second characteristic of objects of wonder is their mysteriousness. Gabriel Marcel has introduced into philosophy a distinction between problem and mystery which is helpful at this point. The province of the mysterious is where the distinction between subject *personal relations are the primary experience*

PROBLEM → MYSTERY

and object breaks down. "A mystery is something in which I am myself involved, and it can therefore only be thought of as a sphere where the distinction between what is in me and what is before me loses its meaning and its initial validity."[5] When I am dealing with a genuine mystery, I cannot get the distance necessary for dealing with it as a pure object, because I cannot totally separate myself from the mystery under contemplation. Marcel quotes with approval a statement by B. P. Jouve: "Mysteries are not truths that lie beyond us; they are truths that comprehend us."[6] If we take as an example the relationship between two people who have loved each other for a long time, the meaning of mystery becomes clearer. Only in a superficial sense can two such persons be totally separated. They are not, in the strict sense, objects for each other, for each has been invaded and shaped by the reality of the other; their beings intermingle. By contrast, in a problematic relationship all the data necessary for objective, verifiable knowledge are before the knowing subject. In a problematic relationship the subject is related to a pure object, because his biographical self is not involved with the object. For instance, a scientist may work on the problem of fly control in a totally objective fashion, because he is not, in any significant existential sense, in a relation of creative interchange with the fly.

Thus, when we say objects of wonder are mysterious we do not mean they are only vaguely known. It is too often assumed that the mysterious is equivalent to the unknown and that, in the light of adequate knowledge, mystery will give way to clarity. Such a view equates mystery and ignorance. Making use of Marcel's understanding of mystery, we can see that the mysteriousness of an object has little to do with how well or how poorly it is known. An object, event, or person may be well understood and adequately explained (in the sense of causal explanation), yet evoke more wonder than a less well-understood phenomenon. For instance, the process of conception, gestation, and birth can be adequately explained, but the event of birth is as productive of wonder for some modern men as it was for the primitive, who somehow vaguely assumed the whole process was caused by the powers of the moon. The more intimately known and ardently loved a place, thing, or person is, the more mysterious it is, be-

Mysterie is something that is contrasted to problems

cause it is so homogenized into the psychological fabric of the knower that knower and known form one reality. By understanding the positive relationship between mystery and knowledge we see the fallacy of the romantic notion that an increase of knowledge leads to an eclipse of wonder. Knowledge destroys mystery and wonder only when it is used hostilely to reduce the dimensions of meaning in an object to those that can be manipulated and controlled.

Presence

The mysterious nature of objects of wonder leads us to consider a third characteristic. If we were to follow a convention which has been introduced by existential philosophy (in particular, Marcel and Buber), we would have to deny that there are *objects* of wonder. Strictly speaking, an object is something thrown over against us, something we can, figuratively, walk around and examine dispassionately in a problematic manner. The other, which we encounter in wonder, is a presence rather than an object (although we shall continue to use the word object in its loose and popular sense), as it involves us in a total cognitive and emotive response.

The notion of presence is as difficult to render precise as it is important. Marcel and Buber have made parallel distinctions which may help us see what is at stake in this notion. Both men distinguish between two primary modes of relating to an object: as a problem or an it, or as a presence or a thou. When Buber speaks of an I-Thou encounter with a tree or Marcel speaks of discovering a presence in a flower, each is indicating a level of experience at which what we normally call an object ceases to be inert and passive. In a wondering encounter the initiative is with the object. The manner in which we are grasped by something that strikes us as wonderful is very unlike the way in which we grasp an object by abstraction, analysis, and categorization. In the wondering encounter the subject is primarily passive, while in the analytical relationship he is active. When, after I have noticed but not relished ninety-nine roses, the one-hundredth suddenly strikes me as an object of wonder, it is *as if* it had taken the initiative and reached out and presented itself to me. Thus, the personal quality of a notion like presence is necessary to describe the experience. In maintaining that a tree may be experienced in wonder as a Thou, Buber does not mean to advocate a panpsychism in which all reality is personal; however, he does mean to suggest that this way of encountering a tree is more like meeting a person than like analyzing an object.

One of the chief characteristics of an encounter between persons is that significant meeting takes place only where each party gives of himself. Persons are, in our experience, those beings who can give and withhold knowledge of themselves. Some knowledge of "objects" has this same quality of interchange. In wonder something gives itself to us. Essential to the task of understanding the significance of wonder which will be pursued throughout this book is an emphasis on the element of *gift* at the primal level of knowledge. It is noteworthy that the word we use to characterize the raw material with which perception deals suggests this person-like, gratuitous quality of knowledge. "Datum" means, literally, what is given. In wonder we are presented with a gift of meaning.

2. SUBJECTIVE ASPECTS OF THE EXPERIENCE OF WONDER

Having described different objects of wonder and some of the formal characteristics they share, we may now turn to the experiencing subject. What are the boundaries of wonder as experienced by the subject? How broadly or narrowly are we to draw them? Perhaps the most adequate way to define the boundaries of any experience is to see them as extending from the original stimulus to the response by which the organism absorbs what has been given. In dealing with wonder we will adopt this method. Thus, we shall trace the *itinerary of the experience of wonder.*

THE STIMULUS AS EXPERIENCED

Surprise

Wonder begins with the element of surprise. The now almost obsolete word "wonderstruck" suggests that wonder breaks into consciousness with a dramatic suddenness that produces amazement or astonishment. We can no more create a state of wonderment than we can plan a surprise for ourselves. Consider, for example, how strange it would be to say, "I'm going out for a walk and wonder at the dogwoods in bloom." It may, indeed, happen that the dogwoods will evoke wonder, but we cannot be assured of it prior to the experience.

Because of the suddenness with which it appears, wonder reduces us momentarily to silence. We associate gaping, breathlessness, bewilderment, and even stupor with wonder, because it jolts us out of the world of common sense in which our language is at home. The language and categories we customarily use to deal with experience are inadequate to the encounter, and hence we are initially immobilized and dumfounded. We are silent before some new dimension of meaning which is being revealed.

Puzzlement

Puzzlement is another ingredient of the initial shock of wonder which can be distinguished for analysis. When something explodes into awareness and shatters our ordinary categories of understanding, it quite naturally creates mental and emotional dis-ease and puzzlement. What is this novel star that has suddenly appeared on my horizon? Who is this stranger who speaks so unexpectedly out of the mouth of my wife? Why is it that the rose I observed yesterday and the day before today confronts me with a miracle of redness? At the same time a new dimension of meaning is revealed, new questions begin to emerge.

Ambivalence

Any experience as traumatic as wonder will arouse a considerable degree of ambivalence. On the one hand, we all fear what is unknown. Of necessity, we order our everyday existence to keep the unexpected and the unexplained to a minimum. In order to get on with the practical requirements of living, we domesticate our world and systematically insulate it against the intrusion of strangeness. When we are wonderstruck our certainties dissolve, and we are precipitated suddenly into contingency. We are like a man waking in the middle of the night in a strange hotel room and not being able, for the moment, to remember where he is. On the other hand, we grow tired of the usual. Unless we are exceptionally gifted with a strong propensity to wonder, the quotidian easily becomes stale and boring. Thus we long for a surprise that will bring refreshment and novelty. A touch of this love of the surprising is probably seen in the sense of expectation with which most of us await the morning mail. Who knows what might come?

The ambivalence connected with wonder is structurally the same as that associated with the experience of the holy. In his classic analysis, *The Idea of the Holy,* Rudolf Otto showed that the holy is always experienced as at once *tremendum* and *fascinans*—as awful, fearful, threateningly powerful, and at the same time fascinating, desirable, promising, and compelling. Wonder partakes of this same ambiguity. Insofar as it disrupts our proven ways of coping with the world, it is menacing; insofar as it offers the promise of renewing novelty, it is desirable and fascinating. If we attend to the strict meanings of the words, we may describe the heart of the experience of wonder as an *awful-promising surprise.*

Admiration

Reality, as it is given to us in wonder, is not only a shock and a surprise, but it is, as Chesterton has said, "a pleasant surprise." It presents itself to us as something having a dignity, worth, meaning, or value which calls forth admiration and appreciation. It is, perhaps, due to the atrophy of the sense of authentic wonder in our culture that we are initally inclined to think of the experience of wonder as at best neutral, or at its worst, horrible. Nevertheless, a phenomenological analysis shows that admiration is inseparable from wonder. If we look at the etymology of the word "admire" we find that it originally meant: to regard with wonder or astonishment or to regard with wondering esteem accompanied by pleasure and delight. The weight of meaning that inheres in the word "admire" in common language reveals the positive value-ful character of wonder. To admire is to celebrate or rejoice in the presence of a thing or a person having some desirable grace, strength, dignity, or other positive value.

The question is frequently asked whether we cannot wonder at something that is horrible. There is a distinct difference between horror and wonder. We are horrified by those things that threaten to degrade or destroy, while we wonder at those things that promise to enrich and fulfill life. Horror and wonder bear the same relation to each other as sacrilege bears to the experience of the sacred. Without an intuition of the sacred there can be no sacrilege; in a similar manner, horror or outrage logically depends upon a prior experience of wonder. One can, for instance, be horrified by Auschwitz or Vietnam only if there has been some prior experience which testifies that human beings are worthy of admiration and appreciation. The experience of horror arises out of the anticipation of violation—and outrage out of the actual violation—of the sense of wonder. It is important to insist upon the priority of wonder, because otherwise we lose the basis of ethics. If there is nothing wonder-ful, nothing that is inviolable and sacred (in principle), then ethics can be based only upon a balance of terror.

Wonder is the foundation of values because a wondering encounter is the basis of a nonutilitarian approach to things and persons. In wonder we experience the other as inexhaustible, as the locus of meanings which are only revealed as we cease to be dominated by the impulse to utilize and possess the other and learn to rejoice in its presence. It is when we cease making imperialistic claims over objects and persons (structurally similar to neurotic claims) and allow them to be what they are in their own right, that we touch the inviolable strangeness which is their sacredness. The intuition of the inviolability or sacredness of objects and persons invests them with the character of mystery—which means merely that they stand out in stark outline as themselves and cannot be reshaped to fit our desires and needs.

Language comes near failing when we try to describe the new density and significance that objects and persons take on when encountered in wonder. This is because, in one sense, wonder adds nothing to our knowledge *about* an object. It is rather that the object comes into focus and is respected and relished in its otherness.

The imagery of apocalypse and resurrection is integral to the experience of wonder. Every wonder-event involves a cognitive crucifixion; it disrupts the system of meanings that secures the identity of the ego. To wonder is to die to the self, to cease imposing categories, and to surrender the self to the object. Such a risk is taken only because there is the promise of a resurrection of meaning. To accept the meaning which is given by the object is to find the world redeemed from drabness or staleness. Refreshment or resurrection leaves us reborn but unable to articulate an adequate testimony. There is nothing new to say about the world ("a rose is a rose is a rose")—only a new ability to celebrate its density and meaning. Kazantzakis' testimony about Zorba illustrates the point well.

He had just what a quill-driver needs for deliverance; the primordial glance which seizes its nourishment arrow-like from on high; the creative artlessness, renewed each morning, which enabled him to see all things constantly as though for the first time, and to bequeath virginity to the eternal quotidian elements of air, ocean, fire, woman, and bread; the sureness of hand, freshness of heart, the gallant daring to tease his own soul; finally, the savage bubbling laugh from a deep, deep wellspring deeper than the bowels of man, a laugh which at critical moments spurted and was able to demolish (did demolish) all the barriers—morality, religion, homeland—which that wretched poltroon, man, had erected around him in order to hobble with full security through his miserable smidgen of life. . . .[7]

RESPONSE TO THE STIMULUS

Turning now to the variety of responses to the stimulus of wonder, we find that we must distinguish between pathological and healthy responses. Since the experience of wonder involves a cognitive and psychological shock, it is necessarily intermittent. We can stand only so much trauma at a time. Pathological responses to wonder are of two types, which will be discussed at length in a later chapter: the effort to seal the ego off against further novelty (the Apollonian pathology) and the effort to live in a continual state of unlimited openness (the Dionysian pathology). At this point our concern is not with pathological responses but with how the healthy personality responds to and integrates the shock of wonder.

Curiosity and Explanation

The first response moves *from puzzlement to curiosity to a search for explanation.*

Although wonder begins in silence, it does not remain forever dumb. As the shock of astonishment wears away, the mind begins to search for some way to dispell the dis-ease. Puzzlement gives way to curiosity, and the search for an explanation begins. This quest begins with the formation of questions.

What is it that has happened?
What does it mean?
Why did it happen?
What is the significance of this wonder-event?
What am I to do in relation to this new dimension of knowledge I have suddenly been given?

In this initial stage of questioning no distinction has yet been made between questions which may be given some objective, verifiable answer and those which may not.

It might be well to coin the word "wonderosity" for this rudimentary state of response in which wonder and curiosity exist in a Siamese twinship. It is not until later that wonder, curiosity, and contemplation become separate activities. This separation seems to take place when the discovery is made that it is possible to get satisfactory answers to some types of questions, and thus alleviate a measure of dis-ease, but not to other types of questions bearing upon the same object. We may, for instance, discover what *causes* the leaves of a tree to be green and its apples red but not *why* it should exist at all. We may trace the process by which a child comes to birth, but we cannot discover why love should bear fruit in such a strange fashion. Some modern philosophers will insist that a question that cannot be answered in principle is no question. Fortunately, however, philosophers cannot legislate what questions may and may not be asked, and we may be relatively certain that human beings will continue not only to be curious about *how* things are but also to wonder *why* they are.

There is a continuous line of development from puzzlement to curiosity to reasoning to scientific investigation. The most notable characteristic of this development is the narrowing down of the area about which questions are asked and the clarification of the questions. Curiosity is the active, heuristic posing of questions. It need not be purely utilitarian in character but may be motivated by a desire for idle knowledge. The inner mental dialogue which arises out of the questions posed by a mind made curious by some puzzling phenomenon is the essence of rational thinking. Curiosity, disciplined, becomes reason. Scientific thought is merely a further development of the questioning process which begins with curiosity and becomes disciplined in reason. The essential difference between reasoning and scientific investigation is the development of a method for deriving answers to questions that are not answered merely by observing. Kant said the essence of science was "putting nature on the rack" and forcing her to answer the questions we desire to have answered by designing experiments to yield knowledge that cannot be gained by observation or contemplation.

The scientific quest for knowledge takes us away from the immediacy of the wonder-producing encounter. The object of scientific thought is not a presence, a thou, or a mystery, but a problem to be solved. The scientist must necessarily abstract elements from the fullness of the concrete object in order to answer the questions he has posed. Let us take as an example Kant's observation that the starry skies without and the moral law within fill us with wonder. The astronomer moves away from the wondering encounter with the stars as he seeks to understand the distance between two stars. His method of solving the problem he has set up will involve an elaborate system of abstractions by which the chemical composition and relative positions of the stars are determined. In this process his relation to the stars shifts from encounter to objectification. The social scientist investigating the cultural factors involved in the creation of conscience undergoes a like switch in relationship to his object. In interviewing a subject, his interest is focused upon the person only as a specimen of moral behavior.

We must beware of assuming that the triumph of a limited relationship between subject and object which is involved in the search for adequate scientific explanation is in any way sinister. One of the shortcomings of existentialist philosophy has been its tendency to underrate the significance of abstraction, objectivity, and problematic thinking. In the open, creative scientist the abstractions and explanations which arise out of the desire to understand and control the world do not prevent a return to the object in a spirit of wonder. Investigation need not destroy respect for the object being studied. Indeed, for the creative thinker, wonder and humility grow in proportion to knowledge. Abstraction is used to deepen knowledge of the concrete, and thus there is a continuing dialectic between investigation and admiration.

Contemplation and Celebration

A second dominant response to the shock of a wonder-event involves the movement from admiration to contemplation to celebration.

If one fundamental impulse in the presence of an awful-promising surprise is to take away the threat by searching for understanding, another impulse is to *enjoy* what is given.

Contemplation is no less a mode of thought or reason than scientific investigation. However, it does differ in both structure and intent. The chief characteristic of contemplation is its receptive passivity. This passivity is not to be confused with inertness or languor but is, rather, the calm and disciplined effort of thought to be open to the uniqueness and novelty of its object. In contemplation, thought makes an effort to be fluid or plastic, to conform itself to its object, and to allow the object to create the categories by which it will be understood. A disciplined silence is essential to contemplation in order to allow the object to speak. The obvious illustration of this type of thought would be the attentive listening involved in trying to understand another person. Marcel suggests another example.

It has been my experience, especially in music, to contrast the work that I appreciate immediately because it fits into special frameworks or schemas that are already there and the work that I only come to love much later but much more deeply because it obliges me to invent new categories for it; it exercises its authority on me, it becomes a centre which imposes on me a regrouping of myself.[8]

In this regard contemplation is the effort to evade the tyranny of the already known—a disciplined attempt on the part of a knower to allow the novel and the unique to create categories that will expand our knowledge.

The passivity implicit in contemplation has been richly dealt with in philosophical and religious literature. Zen Buddhism speaks of a state of "mindlessness" which is necessary for true knowledge. Meister Eckhart, in a similar vein, spoke of the silence and "disinterest" necessary for knowledge of God. More recently, existential philosophers have rediscovered the passive moment in knowledge. Marcel has distinguished between technical and abstract knowledge, which involves an active posing of questions, and secondary reflection, which requires us to "relax in the presence" of the object and make ourselves available to it. Heidegger speaks of the necessity of allowing the object to come across the open toward the knowing subject if truth is to be known. The freedom in which truth is known reveals itself as "the letting-be of what is."

This willingness to stand in a relaxed receptivity before an object involves a certain reverence, epistemological humility, and a willingness to appreciate. These attitudes lie at the heart of contemplation. In contemplation one returns to an object that was given in wonder in order to prolong admiration and appreciation: a favorite stretch of beach, a painting which has already given hours of enjoyment, the face of one long loved, a familiar tree, and so forth. Out of such admiration grows gratitude and the impulse to celebrate, or possibly even to worship. This response, however, brings us to the threshold of the experience of the holy.

3. WONDER, THE HOLY, AND THE VALUABLE

Wonder and awe are closely associated with the experience of the holy. We have already seen that the two experiences are structurally similar: both have as their object a mystery that is at once awful and desirable (*mysterium: tremendum et fascinans*). I will suggest further that there is no substantial difference between wonder and the experience of the holy. The distinction between these two experiences arises only where the forms (linguistic and institutional) in which religious experience is articulated become rigid and a gulf opens between the sacred and the secular. We shall trace this process in a subsequent chapter. For the moment let us concentrate on the phenomenon of the holy as it is known in religious experience.

ONTOLOGIC WONDER AND THE SUBJECT OF RELIGIOUS STATEMENTS

If we approach religious experience by looking at the language of religion, we see that its structure is dual. Just as religious statements consist of a subject and a predicate, religious experience is composed of a primal belief in the existence of a divine dimension of reality or a Divine Being and a secondary conviction that certain events, persons, or objects are revelatory. Thus, for the sake of analysis, we may distinguish between two different types of wonder which are necessary to the constitution of religious experience: ontologic wonder, which is the experiential foundation of belief in the existence of God, and theophanic wonders, which are the experiential basis for the predicates that are assigned to God or the holy.

The foundation of the religious mode of being in the world, no less than of philosophy, is what William James called "ontologic wonder"—the shocking awareness *that* the world exists and does not contain its own explanation. Things are, but they need not have been. In the face of this primal experience of ontologic wonder, two fundamental responses are possible.

1. We may find the mind impotent to discover any adequate explanation for existence, in which case contingency becomes the ultimate philosophical category, and the mind's quest for a sufficient reason is doomed to remain an itch which cannot be scratched.

2. The world may be experienced as demanding a sufficient reason, a noncontingent source beyond itself. It is this second response that forms the basis of the affirmation of the existence of God. The religious way of perceiving the world fuses the ideas of contingency and sufficient reason. The insufficiency of the world leads the mind to posit a sufficient cause; world and God belong together like convex and concave or male and female.

Perhaps the clearest indication of the difference between these two types of response to ontologic wonder is found in the strangely contradictory meanings of the word "contingent." Contingent means both happening-by-chance–accidental–fortuitous and touching–tangential–dependent. When Sartre speaks of the world as contingent, he means it is perceived as existing by chance (it is in this sense that we shall continue to use the word); when theologians speak of contingency, they mean the world is experienced as necessarily dependent upon a source beyond itself.

The religious conviction that arises out of ontologic wonder is not the outcome of an argument or a chain of reasoning but is a basic mode of perception. As Crombie remarks, "The sense of dependence feels not at all like being persuaded by argument, but like seeing. One is not *persuaded* to believe that one is contingent; rather one feels that it is only by persuasion that one could ever believe anything else."[9] It is always possible to cast this mode of perception or affection, which Schleiermacher called "an absolute feeling of dependence," in the form of a logical argument. The arguments for the existence of God which proceed from motion to an unmoved source of motion, or from order to a necessary source for order, are ex post facto efforts to give logical form to the wondering experience of the world as necessitating a sufficient source beyond itself.

We may note in passing the charge made by Sartre, Merleau-Ponty, and others that theology destroys wonder because it eliminates contingency. As Merleau-Ponty states the matter,

For theology recognizes the contingency of human existence only to derive it from a necessary being, that is, to remove it. Theology makes use of philosophic wonder only for the purpose of motivating an affirmation which ends it. Philosophy, on the other hand, arouses us to what is problematic in our own existence and in that of the world, to the point that we shall never be cured of searching for a solution, as Bergson says, "in the notebooks of the master."[10]

If such a charge means only that theology rules out the finality of the categories of chance and accident, it is true, but trivial and uninteresting. If it involves the more radical assumption that to apprehend the world as necessitating a source beyond itself is to cease wondering *that* it exists, it is unproven. A world created by God is no less miraculous or wonderful than one that merely happens by chance. Indeed, it may be that the perception of the world as gift enhances the capacity to celebrate. We shall return to the question of religious and nonreligious modes of expressing the experience of wonder in the final chapter of this book.

WONDERS AND THE PREDICATES OF RELIGIOUS STATEMENTS

Turning now to those revelatory events, objects, or persons which provide us with the predicates of sentences about God or the divine, we discover an inseparable relationship between wonder and theophany. It would be no exaggeration to say that all formative revelatory events are born in wonder. The word "wonder" is frequently used in company with the linguistic family (marvel, portent, miracle, sign) that designates the mode in which the holy is encountered—in which the history, personality, or nature of the God of what Crombie calls "undifferentiated theism" is made known.

In order to understand this relationship we must place ourselves in imagination at the birth point of an original religious experience —that is, an experience in which an existing concept of God or the holy received a new content or predicate. We might as easily choose our example from the central revelatory events of the Judeo-Christian tradition (the Exodus or the Resurrection) as from any number of obscure moments when some sensitive man, now anonymous, has found himself astonished by a holy presence in the life-giving water of a spring or in a rock which provided a place of refuge. All such experiences share the quality of an encounter with what Otto described as a numinous reality which was *mysterium: tremendum et fascinans.* As we have noted earlier, any wonder-event is experienced with great ambivalence, because it both threatens past patterns of valuing and worshiping and promises new patterns.

Let us choose as an example the event of the resurrection of Christ. We have no need, at this point, to discuss what kind of an event it was (subjective, objective, psychological, or historical). The meaning of the event—that is to say, the manner in which the event functioned to provide a new understanding of God—is a matter of historical record which may be examined phenomenologically. At the very least, we may say: in the experience of the events that cluster around the life of Jesus a new vision of the ultimate context of human existence was born. The disciples were themselves unsure about the proper manner in which to talk about the theophany that occurred in Jesus. The plethora of titles given to Jesus (Lord, Messiah, Son of David, Priest of the Order of Melchizedek, New Adam, Lamb of God, Suffering Servant, and so on) is evidence of the playful and poetic extremes to which language had to be stretched to express the happening. If we turn away from the effort to judge the linguistic expressions of the event and examine its functional significance, we shall be able to understand better the total reorientation that any pivotal encounter with the holy requires. In a radically demythologized form the earliest Christian gospel may be stated in the following manner: "Look! Attend! Listen! A child is born, a new being, a new era, a new existential possibility has emerged. Novelty has entered history, and therefore you may be free of the binding illusion that your fate is written in the stars, that you are victims of an order that is determined with no regard for your freedom or care for your being. The fault lies not in your stars but in your own refusal to accept the gracious gift of human freedom. The ground out of which history springs is alive and gracious; therefore anything is possible. Live in openness, wonder, and gratitude, accepting the mysterious gift of the ability to create, act, and forgive!" This gospel pointed out and gave status to a new manner of being in the world that became visible in the theophany of the person of Jesus. Its miraculous character was the new world it created for believers, the total reorientation (conversion, in religious language) it effected.

If we carry our analysis one step further, we may discover the substantial functional identity between the notions of wonder, the holy, and the more modern notion of value. The notion of value springs from an economic metaphor which did not gain philosophical currency until the experience of the market became dominant in the nineteenth century. If we disregard the merely economic understanding, it would seem that what modern man means by value is functionally equivalent to what traditional man meant by the holy. A value is a point of orientation. Eliade has shown that, for archaic man, theophany, or the encounter with the holy, provided an organizational principle for the whole of life. The place of theophany became the *axis mundi,* the central point around which personal identity and the self-understanding of the community was structured. In other words, the encounter with the holy was the basis of what modern man (under impact of the rise of the market place to the center of the village) has begun to call value. It is interesting in this regard to note that in many primitive tribes the objects that were used to store wealth, such as shark's teeth or ceremonial feathers, were of religious significance. Norman Brown says the value attributed to such useless objects, and the prestige conferred on their owner, "is magical, mystical, religious, and comes from the domain of the sacred."[11] Whatever functions to unify life, to assure its meaningfulness, to provide what Tillich called an "ultimate concern" is experienced as *mysterium: tremendum et fascinans.* The wonderful, the holy, and the valuable all share the ability to make men tremble and thus provide an organizing principle for life.

Historically, we have come to a period in Western culture where the wonderful, the holy, and the valuable exist in schizophrenic separation. Wonder is generally reckoned to be an aesthetic emotion, the holy an ecclesiastical monopoly, and value an economic concept.

In subsequent chapters we shall trace something of the history of this division, raising the question of a possible reconciliation.

Unless you turn and become like children, you will never enter the kingdom of heaven.

—MATT. 18:3

There are children playing in the street who could solve some of my top problems in physics, because they have modes of sensory perception that I lost long ago.

—J. ROBERT OPPENHEIMER[1]

CHAPTER II

Childhood
and Wonder

The association of wonder with childhood is so automatic it has become a cliché. The innocent freshness with which children approach the world has long been held up as an ideal state from which the adult is exiled by the relentless tyranny of passing time. Christianity has suggested that salvation involves becoming like a little child; educators and artists have sought means to awaken in adults the spontaneity, curiosity, and sense of delight that seem to be the rule of childish existence. There is almost universal feeling that some of the patterns of perception which are characteristic of childhood must be recaptured if man is to live an authentic life. Such is the conviction that lies in back of the association we automatically make between childhood and the state of wonder.

What exactly do we mean when we speak of the wonder of the child? What does the experience look and taste like? Wonder, in the child, is the capacity for sustained and continued delight, marvel, amazement, and enjoyment. It is the capacity of the child to approach the world as if it were a smörgasbord of potential delights, waiting to be tasted. It is the sense of freshness, anticipation, and openness that rules the life of a healthy child. The world is a surprise party, planned just for me, and my one vocation in life is to enjoy it to the fullest—such is the implicit creed of the wondering child. Reality is a gift, a delight, a surprise—in fact, a toy; it is an excessive, superabundant cafeteria of delights, and should any experience begin to be jaded by boredom and staleness, all one has to do is move on to the next. To wonder is to live in the world of novelty rather than law, of delight rather than obligation, and of the present rather than the future.

In this chapter we shall undertake the exacting task of understanding the structure of childish reasoning and experience which makes the attitude of wonder a possibility. Until this is accomplished we are in no position to discover whether wonder is the same experience in the child as in the adult, or only analogous, and whether or not there is the possibility of a mature type of wonder.

1. THE NATURE OF CHILDISH EXPERIENCE AND REASONING

THE FIRST WORLD OF EXPERIENCE

In the world into which the child is born there are neither subjects nor objects, neither an I nor a thou, because the distinction between the ego and the world is not yet made. It is a fluid world without persons, space, time, or causality, without firm organization or distinct boundaries. For the neonate what we recognize as a separate person—the mother—is only comfort, pleasure, and satisfaction, and the absence of the mother is hunger, want, and discomfort. The neonate recognizes the cause neither of the satisfaction nor the discomfort. He knows delight and discomfort but not their sources. He feels but does not think, and observes but does not yet understand.

It is, of course, impossible for the adult who lives in an ordered world in which interior and exterior are clearly distinguished to think himself back into that stage in life in which all is immediacy and feeling. It is, however, important to realize that what we call reality is, in large measure, a product of personal and corporate construction and is not given ready-made to consciousness. As Cameron suggests, "Each of us has had to build up his own world of reality, and at the same time tie it in functionally with the realities that other persons experience. The apparent firmness and permanence of the external world are in part the projections of our own firm, enduring personality organization."[2]

The motivating factor in the earliest experience of the child is the pleasure principle. He seeks pleasure and avoids discomfort. If mechanistic exactitude is preferred, one may say that the neonate is a bundle of basic instincts seeking satisfaction. Or, with equal accuracy but more poetry, one may say that the quest for delight is the motivating factor in the developing experience of the child. Rooting after a milk-covered nipple may be viewed as an instinctual response to stimulus or as the anticipation and searching out of delight. The child builds up a wider world of reality as he uses his developing reason to explore new pleasurable experiences and to retain the habitual sources of pleasure. The development of reason thus arises out of the quest for pleasure.

THE CONSTRUCTION OF REALITY—THE GROWTH OF REASON

The Meaning of Reason

The aim of reason is to bring order out of chaos—to create a manageable cosmos of meaning out of the multiverse of raw experience. The discovery and creation of order are necessities for human life. Man can live with only so much chaos. Reason constructs a world which is manageable and understood, one from which a measure of strangeness and unpredictability has been banished. It humanizes the world, makes a home out of an environment, and domesticates nature.

This is accomplished by distinguishing, structuring, creating schemata, observing patterns, applying categories, and making judgments. At the heart of reason lies the seeing and/or creation of relations between facts and ideas which are seemingly unconnected in initial experience. Deduction and induction are no more than this. Induction is the art of seeing relations between facts, and deduction is the art of seeing relations between ideas.

Categorical Poverty—the Initial Condition

In the beginning the child has very few categorical needles upon which to knit his experience of the world. Freud's theory of infant sexuality, which is suggestive at this point if not convincing in detail, shows that the earliest experiences of sensual delight, sucking and swallowing, and the converse experience of rejection and spitting out, form response patterns which are manifest in later life in such symbolic ego maneuvers as incorporation, introjection, identification, and rejection. The child is, at first, a mouth, and his oral incorporation of the breast of the mother and other objects in the environment forms his initial way of relating to the exterior world. He quite literally tastes reality and tests it to see whether it is palatable. What promises delight to the taste buds—whether it be the breast, the thumb, or a nearby toy—he seeks to incorporate, to intuit, to take into himself. What is unsatisfying is spit out. Sucking in and spitting out are the primitive forerunners of the many different categories the adult uses to intuit a far richer and more complex world. At this earliest oral stage of development the child has only two categories—what tastes or feels good, hence evokes a happy response, and what does not, and hence calls forth crying, protest, and spitting. Such feelings and responses, primitive though they be, are based upon a primal and semiconscious process of distinguishing and are the roots from which the full-grown tree of reason develops.

Increasing Complexification

As the child grows, his world becomes increasingly complex and demanding. Life is no longer merely milk, cuddling, sleep, and crying. As he becomes more aware of the exterior world, he comes into conflict. He finds that some forms of delight are mutually exclusive. It is not, for instance, possible to have the delight of free bowel action and the delight of Mother's good pleasure at the same time. So the child learns to control himself, to distinguish between situations in which it is "right" to perform an act and those in which it is "wrong." In learning this, he begins to establish a hierarchy of delights, and he learns to control his world to insure the superior ones. His world grows increasingly complex, increasingly structured, but it also offers a wider range of possible delights.

This process of seeing and inventing richer and more comprehensive structures, of apprehending and creating a universe which will satisfy a wide range of desires, is slow indeed. Piaget distinguishes four stages:

1. Up until the age of two to three, reality for the child is solely what is desired.

2. The second stage lasts from two to three until seven to eight. During this time the child lives in two different worlds, one of observation and the other of fantasy and play, and neither world is tested by the criteria of the other. Rather, they are juxtaposed in such a way that the five-year-old can know by observation that cowboys in the contemporary West are ordinary mortals, and yet, in his world of play, "know" equally well that they (and he) kill Indians and bad guys and live romantic lives.

3. Between the ages of seven to twelve these two worlds of play and observation begin to take on a hierarchical arrangement and structure. Imagination and "reality" are more strictly distinguished.

4. From eleven to twelve on, the hierarchy is completed as formal thought and logical rigor begin to develop.[3]

This process is synonymous with the development of reason.

Juxtaposition and Syncretism

As distinguished from adult reasoning, which is either inductive or deductive (leaving aside for the moment the question of pure and practical reason), childish reason has been characterized as transduction. Transduction is constituted by an alternation between the tendency of the child merely to juxtapose facts and judgments which would be seen by the adult as related causally or logically and the alternate tendency to synthesize and homogenize data and judgments which should be separated.

More concrete illustrations of these tendencies might be helpful. Empty the pockets of a five-year-old boy, and you have a mirror of the thought world of the child. His pockets reveal a collection of items—some useful, some merely delightful, and all valuable—with no one item seeming to have anything to do with the next. There are string, a burned-out fuse, a bit of candy (unwrapped and covered with lint—now inedible), two small pine cones, and a genuine imitation sheriff's badge. The thought world of the child is composed of a similar collection of items of experience and knowledge and of feelings and desires which, like a poorly-run museum, lacks any obvious principle of hierarchical organization.

New items are added daily without being catalogued, classified, or related to the other items in the collection. The child juxtaposes items of experience and knowledge which, to the adult mind, involve logical contradiction.

Juxtaposition implies that the child does not see clearly the relations between things or understand the implications of ideas. He sees details but not the whole that is composed of the interrelated details. Piaget illustrates this from the drawings of children.

The child's style and even his thought are therefore comparable to his drawing. A number of details are correctly indicated. The drawing of a bicycle by a child of six, for example, will show, in addition to the frame and the two wheels, the pedals, a chain, a cog-wheel, and a gear. But these details are juxtaposed without any order; the chain is drawn alongside of the cog-wheel instead of being correctly inserted, and the pedals are suspended in mid-aid instead of being fixed. Thus everything happens as though the child really felt the relations in question . . . . But this is as far as his consciousness of relations goes.[4]

What, to the adult, looks like disorder in the juxtaposed world of the child has no such meaning for the child. The child does not feel the discontinuity or the loose-jointed character of his world. On the contrary, he *feels* that everything is connected with everything else; he feels not a deficiency of relations but a superfluity. Piaget defines syncretism as

. . . the spontaneous tendency on the part of children to take things in by means of a comprehensive act of perception instead of by the detection of details, to find immediately and without analysis analogies between words or objects that have nothing to do with each other, to find a reason for every chance event; in a word, it is the tendency to connect everything with everything else.[5]

Syncretism initially appears to run counter to juxtaposition, but it does not, in fact. Insufficient attention to individual items, to details and their relations, leaves the childish mind without a knowledge of the general laws of nature and of thought. "A child knows nothing either of physical necessity (the fact that nature obeys laws) or of logical necessity (the fact that such a proposition necessarily involves such another)."[6] Lacking these general laws which provide adult reason with integrating and ordering principles for dealing with the multiplicity of experienced items, the child must forge ordering principles on the basis of his subjective experience. Thus, the connections he forges between items of experience, the schemata he uses, result from connections that are contingent, fortuitous, and accidental. Things experienced at the same time become associated in the child's mind, and when asked about one of the things, he will explain it in terms of the other. Piaget found that when he asked children of five to six "why the sun did not fall down," their answers merely invoked other features that they associated with the sun—"Because it's hot" or "Because it's yellow."[7] They tended to substitute a description of some quality they associated with the thing for an explanation. The rule of childish reason seems to be this: when two things are given simultaneously in perception, they are fused into a single schema, and this acquires the strength of reciprocal implication.

The Alternating Rhythm

The tendencies toward juxtaposing and syncretizing alternate as the child grows. As Piaget notes,

Syncretism and juxtaposition constitute two phases alternating over indefinite periods in the mind of the child . . . . Sometimes the child builds up new general schemas, tries to connect everything, and tries to incorporate the new and unexpected elements into the old, accustomed framework. At other times the discovery or the sudden emergence of unclassifiable and incomprehensible phenomena will burst these frameworks and dissolve the schemas until new systems are formed, only to be destroyed in turn.[8]

As this rhythmic process continues throughout childhood, there is a progressive clarification both of the nature of the individual items of experience and of the tissue of relationships that join them. Greater attention to detail reveals more accurately the objective relationships that exist between individual objects, and as more objective schemata of interpretation are built up the child is less captive to his subjective, unsocialized feelings about things.

It is crucial that this process of the deepening and widening of experience be recognized, for it suggests that the individual atoms which compose experience of the world of nature, society, and personality are seen clearly and objectively only as general patterns of interpretation are developed. The growth of reason, the patterning and structuring principle, coincides with deeper and clearer immersion in the world of individuals. The implications of this for wonder will be seen shortly.

This continual oscillation between the individual atomic units of experience and the schemata that organize these units into a meaningful totality is the normal process of development in the child. Indeed, in the healthy and open adult this same process continues to operate at a diminishing rate of frequency as the schemata grow more adequate to interpret the kaleidoscope of experienced reality. It is all too common, however, for the patterns and schemata which have been created as means to understand individual atoms of experience to solidify and become substitutes for experience of concrete reality. When this happens, the child (or the adult) stagnates and closes his mind against the intrusion of wonder. Instead of using reason to interpret experience, he uses it to prevent the inbreaking of new experiences. The attitude is too well known to need much comment—"Don't confuse me with the facts; my mind is made up." When this essential rhythm of thought breaks down, the wonder-producing contact with the strange and the novel ceases, and thought then proceeds not on the basis of present experience but on past formulations of experience.

This tendency to alternate between juxtaposing and syncretizing is rooted in the egocentric character of childish thought, which lacks awareness of the viewpoints of others. The child is as unconscious of his own thought as he is of the thought of others. He does not reflect upon his own thought processes; he does not look at himself from the point of view of others; his mind is not yet socialized. Self-consciousness always arises in dialogue with other-consciousnes, the knowledge of the I with the knowledge of the thou. The child only gradually grows out of the state of immediacy into self-consciousness. It is contact with the world and with other persons that gives birth to reflective self-consciousness. In immediacy there is absolute certainty. Only when the mind has undergone the abrasive intercourse with other minds and viewpoints does doubt arise. It is then forced to verify and defend its conclusions.

2. SOME IMPLICATIONS OF CHILDISH REASON FOR WONDER

Although I have given only the barest outline of the structures of childish thought, we have seen enough to get some clues about the meaning of the phenomenon of wonder in children.

IMMEDIACY

There is an old Chinese proverb which captures the immediate character of childish thought: "Only to a child is pure happiness possible. Later it is always tainted with the knowledge that it will not last." The child accepts what is given in the moment with little thought of what it implies. His enjoyment is not burdened with the awareness that no good thing or bad thing lasts forever. For the adult the awareness of the passing of time casts a veil of reluctance, of hesitation, over the experience of immediate enjoyment. Certainly the child does have some remembrance of the past and some anticipation of the future, but the primary mode of time in which he lives is the present. Immediate enjoyment, delight in the presence of ———, is but another way of describing the experience of wonder in one of its aspects.

When we speak of the innocence of a child, it is this quality of immediacy, of spontaneous enjoyment, that we signify. No adult can be innocent in this sense, for the immediacy of the child results from his relative lack of experience and from the small number of past connotations and future expectations which he brings to burden new experience. In encountering a dog for the first time, a child approaches the experience with neutral expectations (unless his parents have created a sense of anxiety in him about novelty); he is ready to meet the dog on its own terms. Later, when his experience of dogs is greater, he will approach each new dog with fears or expectations arising out of his previous encounters. For better or for worse, the adult can never go back to the type of wonder that arises on first seeing a thing.

Even if it proves possible to revivify jaded vision, to learn to see things freshly, it is not possible for the adult to recapture the innocence of first sight.

LACK OF NECESSITY

In looking at the foundational tendencies of childish thought, juxtaposition and syncretism, we saw that the child does not see his world as law-governed. Piaget sums this up: "Juxtaposition is after all the sign of the complete absence of necessity from the thought of the child."[9] This means the child lives in a world that is contingent; anything can happen, as far as he is concerned, because he is not yet aware of the law-abiding character of nature or the logical necessity involved in thought and language. In his loose-jointed world, the wildest type of novelty is possible. It would not be wide of the mark to say that the child's vision of the world is like Sartre's, with the exception that the child experiences contingency with delight rather than nausea. It is conceivable in the child's world that when he opens his mouth a snake rather than a tongue will appear, but the child's reaction is to relish the possibility of such novelty—not to resent it.

We might make the same point by saying that the world of the child is one of imagination rather than logic, of fantasy rather than fact, of play rather than work. In imagination and play, the rules of the game can change. The only laws governing play are those that are made up and adhered to as long as the game gives delight. Thus, the laws of the world of the child can all be broken. Necessity is created only to provide a structure within which delight may be experienced. When the delight wanes, the necessity is destroyed. When it gets boring to follow the rule that all prisoners must stay in jail until somebody from their side touches base, then the rules are changed. The child tends to think in terms of the logic of play about the whole world. If a pet dies, Daddy can bring it back to life, or the doctor can. If no child is allowed up when the company arrives (understood to be an inflexible rule, of the same order as the rule of death and other laws of nature), this, the child thinks, does not really apply to "me." There is, for the child, no necessary law that cannot be changed to fit the deepest desires and demands of the heart.

Because the idea of necessity is lacking from the child's world orientation, he escapes much of the sense of *staleness* that arises in the law-governed and necessary world of the adult. A strange reaction sets in when the adult mind is confronted with law-governed regularity. Those "natural" sequences which we come to think of as law-abiding (the rising and setting of the sun, the rhythm of the seasons, the cycle of birth, maturation, and death, and so on—that is, those things that occur with regularity) soon lose their marvelous character for the adult. What is regular (literally rule-governed or rule-abiding) comes to be familiar, and what is familiar, contemptible. It is a strange and tragic fact that we grow bored with what is familiar, with what can be calculated, measured, and predicted—with what seems to the jaded mind as inevitable and necessary. The specter of necessity throws a pall over the adult mind.

Each year I anticipate the arrival of the violets in the spring, knowing they will come because they always have—because the regularity of natural processes will bring them forth this year as it did last year. When they bloom I look at them with some sense of pleasure, my anticipation satisfied. The reaction of my daughter is entirely of another kind. The surprise of first finding violets is repeated each year, the discovery remade, and delight produced anew by the surprising discovery that suddenly, apart from any expectation—without being compelled to bloom by necessity of nature—unannounced, the violets have arrived.

It is perhaps this lack of a sense of necessity that allows the child to enjoy again and again a game, a song, a story, or merely the repetition of a word. The child is familiar without being bored. Chesterton observes,

A child kicks his legs rhythmically through excess, not absence of life. Because children have abounding vitality, because they are in spirit fierce and free, therefore they want things repeated and unchanged. They always say, "Do it again"; and the grown-up person does it again until he is nearly dead. For grown-up people are not strong enough to exult in monotony.[10]

A world where succeeding similar experiences are juxtaposed allows each of the experiences to be savored for itself rather than being subsumed under some general category. The thought world of the child does not show an inner synthesis in which the elements are necessarily related to each other.

CONCRETENESS

Piaget observes that when a seven-year-old is asked why he knows the sun is alive he answers, "Because it moves," but he never appeals to some general proposition, such as "All things that move are alive." He concludes that the reasoning of a child (up to eleven to twelve) is concerned with particulars, with individual cases, and does not reach the level of generality.[11] The juxtaposed world of the child is a world of particulars bound together by only the most tenuous and subjective feelings of relationship. Violets are more real than flowers, robins than birds, and the concrete than the abstract.

This characteristic of childish thought links it up with wonder. One type of wonder is the reaction to a particular experienced in its uniqueness and singularity. As long as I remain in an attitude in which I greet each dapple-brown bird by identifying it as merely another English sparrow, I miss seeing the marvel that any particular sparrow is.

INTIMACY

Just as the distinction between subject and object, inside and outside, is not clearly made in the world of childish thought, likewise there is an indistinct border between the personal and the impersonal. The child's world is highly personalized and intimate; it is more like him than unlike him. Thus, feelings may be attributed to objects. Landscapes may be happy or sad and animals good or bad. Milk that spills may be scolded for its malevolent intent and chairs kicked for their propensity to trip innocent toddlers. The neutrality and impersonality of objects becomes obvious only as the child passes into the closing phases of transductive thought.

We may also note that a child is a natural existentialist. His world is perceived more as a utensil than an object, more as *zuhanden* than as *vorhanden* in Heidegger's terms. It is seen primarily in terms of its immediate relevance: a chair is for sitting;

marbles are for shooting; and other children are either friends or enemies, depending upon how they fit into the game being played at the moment.

The similarity of the child's experience of the intimate and personal character of the world and the experience of wonder is clear. While the adult has passed through the stage of abstraction and objectification, in wonder he receives the world back as a gift that is presented to him in a quasi-personal matter. It is only degraded intelligence that completely depersonalizes the world and deals with it solely as an it.

MASTERY, ACTION, AND WONDER

The developing world of the child is not primarily one of contemplation and thought but one of action. The development of reason, the ability to structure and distinguish, is primarily the outcome of the child's effort to cope with the world—to master it. Hence, it is important to isolate the relation between activity and wonder in the child.

For the healthy child, novelty presents a challenge to mastery. Much of the process of getting experience of an ever widening world consists of learning to cope with strange objects and novel situations. The child's world is one which is constantly being invaded by novelty—a strange, furry beast that barks and wags its tail, new toys, new playmates, new neighborhoods, and so on. Each of these new situations presents a challenge to the child. In order to be comfortable in the presence of novelty he must know what he is to *do* and how he is to *act* in the new situation— how he is to cope with it.

Novel objects and situations are experienced as delightful by the child only when he is convinced there is some appropriate form of action he can take or when he understands that no action on his part is called for. A novel situation with which the child feels impotent to cope is experienced as frightful and paralyzing and not as delightful. In her study of normal children, Lois Murphy, in regard to novel situations, says:

At first the response of the majority was simply to stand and stare . . . then to an initial exploration to collect data for appraisal of the scope of the opportunity. The most daring children explored their own capacities and limits by trying things out; when they found themselves involved in something they could not manage, they shifted to something which was within their ability. The paralysis in new situations shown by some children suggested that the stress involved not knowing what to do.[12]

The child who meets a new situation with which he feels unable to cope, either because his parents have trained him to be anxious in the presence of novelty or because the situation is realistically beyond the range of his powers of mastery, tends to withdraw either with a feeling of defeat or one of unconcern. The normal child will merely turn his attention to some other source of enjoyment with which he can cope. The autistic child, on the other hand, will tend to become detached and defeated, and in time will be unable to find anything to give him delight. Continued impotence to cope, either real or imaginary, produces listlessness and drives out the sense of wonder and delight. In fact the autistic child, like the sociopath, seems to experience neither end of the emotional spectrum—neither wonder nor disgust, and neither delight nor fear.

The range within which novelty is experienced as delightful is limited, on the one hand, by a challenge to action which the child feels he cannot handle and, on the other hand, by a situation he feels he has completely mastered. Lois Murphy reports the following sequence in the child's dealing with newness:

Anxiety about the new stimulus-situation or demand gives way to interest as familiarization begins. Increasing mastery is accompanied by increasing zest and gratifying repetition. As the activity and object become totally mastered—where there is nothing more that is new, nothing new at all—interest wanes. The child's attention turns to a new challenge.[13]

Both the completely unfamiliar (hence, unmanageable) and the unchallenging (hence uninteresting) fall outside the range of wonder for the child.

3. CONCLUSIONS

The process of the development of reason proceeds from the initial condition of loose-jointed categorical poverty, in which the world is interpreted largely in terms of feeling and desire, to a state of relative objectivity about the age of eleven to twelve, at which time the child becomes capable of formal reasoning. At no time is the child's mind a *tabula rasa* upon which experience imprints itself. The gaining of experience is inseparable from experimentation, structuring, categorizing, and judging. Thus, the intuiting of an ever widening world, the delight of new experience, is bound up with the growth of reason.

It has been widely suggested by romanticism and some forms of existentialism that the process of abstracting, judging, reasoning, is somehow the villain responsible for the loss of wonder. If the child's experience of wonder and delight is any criterion, nothing could be further from the truth.

For the child, the growing ability to reason is correlated with a growing sense of wonder about the world that reason enables him to discover. Wonder is no more dissolved by reason than freedom by law or enjoyment by discipline. We must look for the causes underlying the loss of a sense of wonder and delight, not in the activity of reasoning, but rather in the attitude in which the activity is carried out.

Nothing in the normal process of the development of reason in a child automatically leads to the eclipse of wonder. Children in whom reason does not develop—the so-called "wolf children," for instance—evidence bafflement and a low degree of delight and wonder. We shall also see that in primitive society there is growth into socialized maturity without the high degree of loss of wonder that we find in Western technological society. Even in our complex society we find that some adults have retained the sense of wonder and tend to live highly creative lives, yet have a better-than-average grasp of reality. All of these facts suggest that, contrary to the romantic assumption, there is nothing in increasing knowledge that makes inevitable the eclipse of wonder.

The sense of delight in the child is bound up with the possibility of action, mastery, and control. The mastery of novelty is one of the most constant sources of childhood delight and wonder. One might almost measure the psychic health of a child by the number of times his eyes sparkle with the triumphant affirmation: "I did it! I did it!"

This fact of childish experience runs contrary to many of the suggestions which locate the causes of the loss of wonder in the activity of controlling, mastering, and manipulating the world. Technology, utilization, and the effort to control—these have all been widely indicted and pronounced guilty of destroying wonder. D. H. Lawrence might be singled out as an example of this anti-technological attitude. Yet the experience of children points to the linking of mastery and wonder. It is not the effort to control but the *assumption* that one has completely mastered that leads to the loss of zest and delight.

If, as I have suggested, nothing intrinsic to the growth of reason or the ability to act appropriately necessitates an eclipse of the attitude of wonder, why does the end of wonder so often coincide with the beginning of adult life in our culture? Why does the child stop wondering?

It may be extremely difficult to *explain* the eclipse of wonder. It is not difficult to *describe* how it happens.

Unlike some varieties of bees who come into the world to find that the previous generation has disappeared and left them only a store of food, human infants are raised by parents. And parents very often have ceased to wonder. Parents who are anxious about novelty communicate this attitude to their children: the world is to be suspected of being guilty and hostile until it proves itself otherwise. Needless to say, when a child adopts this attitude, the world seldom has a chance to prove its innocence.

In like manner, many parents create in the child a sense of impotence to cope with novelty because of their own timidity and sense of failure. A child who reflects his parents' impotent judgment of themselves will approach experience with a built-in attitude of defeat and timidity. Novelty will be experienced not primarily as something promising delight, but as something that threatens the limited coping powers in which the child feels secure.

Another way parents force an eclipse of wonder is by forcing children too rapidly out of the world of play into the world of work. Children who are pushed to succeed in the utilitarian world too quickly are prematurely forced out of the natural environment of childhood—play, imagination, and leisure. In the world of total utility, curiosity is cultivated because of its pragmatic value in posing problems that can be given definite answers. On the other hand, wonder may appear pointless and impractical. It seems sensible and useful to wonder *how* a bear finds a honey tree, for such curiosity might lead to a budding interest in nature and a career as a naturalist. But what sense does it make to wonder *that* a bear likes honey, as Pooh does:

> Isn't it funny
> How a bear likes honey.
> Buz, buz, buz.
> I wonder why he does?[14]

To wonder *that* there should be such things as honey and bears— and people to delight in them—is a strange and unproductive attitude in a strictly utilitarian world.

The underlying reason for the eclipse of wonder must be sought in the basic attitudes toward life and the fundamental models of man adopted by those who educate the wonder out of children. The explanation for the loss does not lie in a genetic approach to the experience of children, but will be found, rather, in study of the pathology of adult experience.

Twinkle, twinkle, little star,
How I wonder what you are!

He [the Bushman] had an extraordinary relationship with the stars . . .
I had a wonderful illustration of this on my way out of the desert. I
walked away from our campfire one night to go to the camp of the
Bushmen to talk with them for the last time. Halfway between I saw
against the star sheen the figure of something. It was a woman, holding a child up to the stars and saying something. I whispered to my
interpreter, "What's going on?" He said to me, "Well, that woman,
she's asking the stars up there to take away from this child the heart
of a child and give him the heart of a star." "Why the heart of a star?"
"Because the stars are great hunters and she wants her little boy to
have the heart of a hunter."

—LAURENS VAN DER POST[1]

The starry sky . . . from Plato to the Stoics was the purest embodiment
of reason in the cosmic hierarchy, the paradigm of intelligibility and
therefore of the divine nature of reality as such.

—HANS JONAS[2]

Now when Jesus was born in Bethlehem of Judea in the days of Herod
the king, behold, wise men from the East came to Jerusalem, saying,
"Where is he who has been born king of the Jews? For we have seen
his star in the East, and have come to worship him."

—MATT. 2:1–2

Two things fill the mind with ever new and increasing admiration and
awe, the oftener and more steadily we reflect on them: the starry
heavens above me and the moral law within me.

—IMMANUEL KANT[3]

Twinkle, twinkle, little star,
How I wonder what you are!

CHAPTER III

The Wonder-ful Cosmos of Traditional Man

The crisis in self-understanding through which Western man is now passing is most clearly visible when we contrast the world views and foundational attitudes and values of traditional and modern cultures. Our study will suggest that traditional man may best be understood as *homo admirans*—wondering man. He accepted his life and his environment as a meaningful gift which filled him with admiration and gratitude, and responded actively by creating a community in harmony with patterns of meaning and value which he believed were homogenized into the cosmos. By contrast, modern man increasingly experiences himself, in anxiety, as the sole value-creating force in what is still called a uni-verse but what for many has become a chaotic multi-verse, devoid of intrinsic meaning.

Implicit in phrases such as "foundational attitudes and values" and "traditional man" is the assumption that there is sufficient unity underlying the diverse mythological, philosophical, and theological symbols used in the premodern world to constitute *a* world view. This assumption will be supported by showing that pivotal myths of archaic man, philosophical expressions of the Greek mind, and theological doctrines of the Hebrew-Christian tradition agree in considering wonder a necessary ingredient of authentic life.

1. PRIMAL MAN—MYTH AND WONDER

The idea of wonder was not formally spelled out in the Western tradition until the Greeks discovered that it was the foundation of philosophical thought. Nevertheless, the phenomenon of wonder is as old as mankind, for it is the attitude that marks man's awareness that he is in the presence of the holy. Since we are unable to isolate the concept of wonder in the inexactly differentiated experience of primal man, we must discover it indirectly by looking at the total primal vision of the world. In the mythological language of primal man we shall find recommended certain basic stances toward life which are identical with stances later explicitly associated with the idea of wonder. In the beginning is wonder—but we must look behind the dramatic, concrete images and stories of primal man to discover it.

Who is primal man? We might equally well speak of primitive, aboriginal, tribal, pretechnological, or archaic man. Regardless of what term we use, we shall be referring to tribal peoples who lived before industry and commerce changed the face of the earth, and to those contemporary primitives who continue to live apart from the determining currents of twentieth-century life.

We may now preview the argument I shall be developing. Any human being who looks at the world without putting on overly distorting ideological glasses finds a checkerboard of pleasure and pain, good and evil, light and darkness, harmony and disorder—life-giving and life-destroying forces. This twofold character of fundamental experience which is common to all men will be represented here by the symbols cosmos and chaos. The world of primal man was, first, a cosmos, an ordered and ordering totality having a positive meaning and value. The perception of the world as cosmos elicited responses of wonder, admiration, and gratitude. However, to the degree that the world of primal man was filled with irregularities that threatened life, it was perceived as chaos, and ceremonial, magical, religious, ritualistic, scientific, and pragmatic ways of acting were devised to domesticate the chaos and reduce disorder to tolerable proportions.

THE WORLD AS COSMOS

The idea that the world is a cosmos contains at least three inter-related affirmations which must be separated for analysis: reality is a unified totality; its harmony is complex and rhythmic; and some sacred power creative of value is at work at the heart of nature, man, and society.

The Unity of the Cosmos

Primal man knew little of the hard-and-fast distinctions that Western thought has come to make between the animate and the inanimate, the natural and the supernatural, the material and the mental, the secular and the religious, or the factual and the symbolic. The chief rule of life was continuity rather than discontinuity; men, stars, animals, and gods were all related in a family way: all things were bound together in the economy of the cosmos. In speaking about African religion, John Taylor has noted:

Cosmic oneness is an essential feature of primal religion. Not only is there less separation between subject and object, between self and non-self, but fundamentally all things share the same nature and the same interaction one upon another—rocks and forest trees, beasts and serpents, the power of the wind and waves upon a ship, the power of a drum over a dancer's body, . . . the living, the dead, and the first ancestors, from the stone to the divinities a hierarchy of power but not of being, for all are one, all are here, all are now.[4]

Primal man did not express this vision of unity in formal philosophical terms. He did not speak of the problem of the one and the many, of being and becoming, or of appearance and reality, as Greek philosophers did. His myths and stories, however, were saturated with the conviction that there was unity in diversity and that kinship was the fundamental fact of reality. One example of this was the idea of *mana* (a Polynesian concept that there is a humanlike force or agency in all things), which was widespread in primal cultures. To say that all things had *mana* was a concrete way of affirming that at all levels of reality the same principle or power functioned as they knew in human life.

Just as all life shared a common potency, it also shared the fundamental duality which was found in human existence. Like man, the universe also was composed of male and female elements. The active could not survive without the passive, the sun without the moon, or the sky without the earth. All productivity was the result of the coming together of the male and the female; hence the common practice of having both male and female deities in the pantheons of primal theologies.

A dramatic illustration of the unity of the cosmos is contained in the idea, almost universally present in primal myths, that man is a microcosm, reflecting and participating in the same principles and powers that make a cosmos of the world. This same idea, which was richly developed in the Greek concept of man as a *logos* being and in Renaissance humanism, is expressed in literal and pictorial terms in Hopi thought:

> The living body of man and the living body of the earth were constructed in the same way. Through each ran an axis, man's axis being the backbone, the vertebral column which controlled the equilibrium of his movements and functions. Along this axis were several vibratory centers which echoed the primordial sound of life throughout the universe or sounded a warning if anything went wrong.[5]

Life for the primal man, then, was one. His environment was not a neutral envelope but a cosmos having the same structure and potency as he experienced in himself.

The Harmony of the Cosmos

The unity of the cosmos of archaic man was a unity within multiplicity, a diversity bound together in a rhythmic harmony. Ultimate reality was not the static perfection of the Prime Mover but a continual dance, uniting seeming opposites. For primal man the drama of the recurring seasons provided the organizing model for interpreting the whole of reality. In the rhythm of the seasons, summer and winter, light and darkness, creation and destruction, and life and death were united in a moving harmony. This harmony of opposites applied as much to man as to nature, as the Hopi myth of the road of life illustrates.

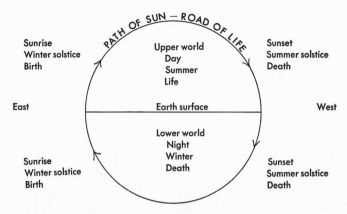

As Waters comments on this view,

Also like the sun, man travels west at death to re-enter the *sipa-puni* [the place of emergence into this world] and return to the world below. Here he is reborn, like a baby, to live another stage of existence in the same great cycle. Life and death, then, are considered not as two separate stages completing mankind's temporal and post-earthly existence, but as complementary phases in an ever-recurring cycle; a continuity that remains unbroken until mankind passes through the seven successive worlds.[6]

By interpreting human destiny on the model of the rhythmic renewal of nature, primal man asserted his faith in the supremacy of life over death; he affirmed that the cosmos was trustworthy and was adequate to preserve, support, and renew life. All of the bitter experiences which could be summarized by the symbolism of darkness—suffering, illness, death, and tragedy—could thus be faced with the confidence that, in the economy of the cosmos, light arose out of darkness and life out of death, just as spring emerged yearly from the deadly barrenness of winter. The testimony of the seasons was certain—death did not have final dominion; it was an episode in the story of life and not its conclusion.

Cosmos and Value

The unity, order, and rhythm evident in the cosmos were not, for primal man, merely neutral facts or what modern man considers "laws" of nature which must be given meaning and value by man. Fact, meaning, and value were not separated. While modern man tends to think of value and meaning as imposed upon objects by the subject, primal man assumed there was an objective meaning immanent within the cosmic process. The cosmos did not merely exist—it meant something; it evidenced a purpose, an end (*telos,* as Greek philosophers were later to say). The rhythmic harmony existed in order to preserve and enrich life.

Of course, primal man did not talk about "meaning" and "value." As we noted earlier, the idea of value is a metaphor taken from the world of commerce and did not enter prominently into philosophical thought until after the industrial revolution. Primal man made his affirmations about the world with familiar and concrete images. One of the most common images, in which we can see an affirmation of the "value" of the cosmic process, was that of the earth as "mother." To speak of "Mother Earth" reflected the belief that the ultimate matrix of life was nurturing and not merely neutral. Again, to illustrate from the Hopi world view:

With the pristine wisdom granted them, they understood that the earth was a living entity like themselves. She was their mother; they were made from her flesh; they suckled at her breast. For her milk was the grass upon which all animals grazed and the corn which had been created specially to supply food for mankind. But the corn plant was also a living entity with a body similar to man's in many respects, and the people built its flesh into their own. Hence corn was also their mother. Thus they knew their mother in two aspects which were often synonymous—as Mother Earth and as the Corn Mother. . . .[7]

If we were to conceptualize the feeling for existence expressed in this metaphor, we might say that the highest categories primal man used were nurture, succor, and gift. Human existence was not a weed that sprang accidentally out of barren soil, but a gift which was nurtured by the cosmos.

The highest expression of archaic man's confidence that the cosmos was a living, value-creating process was in his theology. Gods, goddesses, and helping spirits were everywhere waiting to aid those believers who served them well. One characteristic of all tribal religion was the conviction that the gods, or at least an important and eventually triumphant majority of them, had singled out The People for special attention and concern. Needless to say, each tribe considered itself The People. The gods gave The People their existence, their history, and the rudiments of their culture. Their benevolence was obvious in the food that sprang from the earth as well as in the social organization that governed the tribe.

THE WORLD AS CHAOS

Although primal man lived with the dominant conviction that reality was a cosmos, he nevertheless saw clearly that chaos was always present or threatening. While the seasons passed with calculable and life-giving regularity, there were the irregularities and accidents that threatened the order necessary to the maintenance of life. Storms, droughts, unexplained failures of crops, conquest by "heathen" tribes who were enemies of The People, disease, and accidental death periodically interrupted the orderly course of events. Nature may have been motherly—she may have succored and nourished life with her rhythms—but she also brought decay, disease, and death.

The power of chaos became incarnate for the primal imagination in the figures of demons, witches, evil spirits. and occasional devils. In early Semitic thought chaos was symbolized by the might of the sea, which was always endangering the ordered life of those who lived on the land. As long as chaos could be rendered concrete by the imagination, appropriate action could be devised for dealing with it. For instance, a holy war could be waged against neighboring tribes who were agents of chaos, and evil spirits could be warded off with the proper liturgical services. In short, while chaos could not be eliminated, it could be domesticated.

The surprising thing is that primal man was not led by the negativities of existence to conclude that chaos was the final truth and cosmos merely an illusion. He knew more of evil and disease than modern man, but was still able to maintain basic trust in the superiority of the sacred force that worked in man and nature to create a cosmos. Demons, devils, witches, and evil spirits may have been abroad in the land, but their power was limited and was finally under the dominion of the forces that sustained life. The last word for primal man was not despair in the face of chaos but hope in the presence of cosmos.

RESPONSES TO COSMOS AND CHAOS

There are two types of responses with which we are concerned —feeling or attitudinal responses and active responses. How did primal man *feel* about his world, and how did he *act* in relation to it?

Attitudinal Responses

We have seen that primal man lived in a world filled with objects and events which were sacred or holy. We may, thus, assume that wonder and awe were prevalent feeling-responses of primal man. The world, being sacral, was a strange and mysterious place. While this feeling was characteristic of all pretechnological cultures, there was another, seemingly opposite feeling-response which was no less typical—the feeling of *intimacy*. The world was strange and mysterious, but it was, nevertheless, a *home*. Primal man responded to the conviction of the unity of the cosmos with the feeling of intimate belonging. Man was not a stranger and intruder in some alien sphere called "nature"; he was a part of all that was. Laurens Van der Post illustrates this feeling in commenting on the world view of the African Bushmen.

This first man lived in an extraordinary intimacy with nature. There was nowhere that he did not feel he belonged. He had, from my observation, he has, I will say, none of that dreadful sense of not belonging, of isolation, of meaninglessness which so devastates the heart of modern man. Wherever he went he felt that he belonged, and, what was more important, wherever he went he felt that he was known. We today are convinced that we know. We are a generation of know-alls. But few of us have the life-giving feeling of being known. Wherever this little man went he was known. The trees knew him; animals knew him as he knew them; the stars knew him. His sense of relationship was so vivid that he could speak of "our brother the vulture." He looked up at the stars and he spoke of

"Grandmother Sirius" and of "Grandfather Canis" because this was the highest title of honor he could bestow.[8]

It is one of the ironies of history that when the continuity of all life was finally established on a scientific basis by the work of Darwin and others, when man's kinship with nature was demonstrated, Western man had ceased to feel this kinship. The affirmation of the continuity of animal and human life was not new with Darwin; it was a part of the credo of every primal theology. However, the spiritual atmosphere in which Darwin demonstrated this continuity was vastly different from that of a primal culture. By the nineteenth century, Western man had come to stake his claim to dignity not on being a part of a natural order, a cosmos, or even the kingdom of God, but on being above the natural order. He thought of himself as being related to nature not as a brother but as a lord—not in the spirit of cooperation and thankfulness but in the spirit of domination. For primal man, however, belief in the continuity of all life resulted in a feeling of intimate belonging—of being at home in the world, even as it remained mysterious, sacred, and unpredictable.

Gratitude was a central feeling-response of primal man. Almost without exception, festivals involving sacrifice, communion, and thanksgiving were integral to archaic culture. Some modern thinkers whose hostility toward the sacred is a point of honor have maintained that all sacrifice arises out of fear and the desire to buy off the gods, and that what seems to be gratitude and thanksgiving is merely the result of guilt. The only answer to such a reductionistic attempt to turn every thanksgiving into a festival of fear and guilt and every sacrifice into an effort to manipulate and destroy by giving, is to expose it to the light of day and allow it to vanish. Fear and the desire to propitiate the gods certainly entered into primal rites of sacrifice and communion, as they do into the modern-day equivalents. However, it would be unrealistically cynical to suppose that real gratitude was absent. Malinowski has suggested that primitive man sacralized food because he saw it as a token of the beneficence of nature. In receiving food from nature primitive man felt the forces of destiny and Providence, and it was for this reason that he shared his food sacrificially with his spirits and divinities. Of the primitive attitude toward food, Malinowski says, "We can see in it the germs of what in higher types of religion will develop into the feeling of dependence upon Providence, of gratitude, and of confidence in it."[9]

Active Responses

Perhaps the best way to characterize primal man's active response to the sacral world in which he lived is to say that he was governed by a *spirit of cooperation*. His life was defined with nature rather than against her. So long as he observed the practical and ceremonial rules governing planting, fishing, and hunting, he had every confidence that nature would care for him.

One manner of cooperating with nature was to pattern all significant action after archetypes that were revealed in the cosmos or in the history of The People. When primitive man made a house or a city, he modeled it after the image of the cosmos; when he performed a ceremony he did it just as it was done at the beginning of time by the gods or heroes. When, for instance, Navahos are asked why something is done in a particular way, they answer, "Because the Holy People did it that way in the first place." As Eliade says, archaic man "cosmicized" himself.

Another way of cooperating with those forces in the cosmos which control chaos was by ceremonial reenactment of the primal victory of the gods. A common element in primal myths was the story of the creation of the world, in which the forces of chaos were destroyed by the creator gods. Each year this victory over chaos had to be reenacted in order to insure the continuance of the victory for the coming year. The Persian form of this myth is typical:

On the last day of the year the universe was dissolved in the primordial waters. The marine monster Tiamat—symbol of darkness, of the formless, the non-manifest—revived and once again threatened. The world that had existed for a whole year *really* disappeared. Since Tiamat was again present, the cosmos was annulled; and Marduk was obliged to create it once again, after having once again conquered Tiamat.[10]

The new year's festivals, in which this or a similar myth was ceremonially relived, were primal man's way of becoming contemporary with the cosmogony and pledging his allegiance to the forces that created order, meaning, and value.

When ceremonial participation in the cosmicizing forces is seen as a way of pledging allegiance, there is no great gulf between celebration in a liturgical or magical manner and those forms of action which we prefer to designate as pragmatic, practical, or scientific. Primal science and practical wisdom devised medicines for the cure of disease, fertilizers for crops, and a whole body of knowledge for insuring the health and food supply of the tribe. However, the ceremonial and the practical were both means of cooperating with the wisdom of nature. Celebration and manipulation could not be separated in the primal world view any more than faith and works can be separated in the Judeo-Christian view of man. Action that is authentic must be appropriate to its context, and finally—for the religious man, primal or modern—the actions by which we humanize and give value to the world arise out of, participate in, and are of a piece with forces and powers which are more than human. Even in acting and in taking responsibility, man is not alone. He cooperates with cosmicizing powers which are everywhere operative. This is the source of his dignity and assurance.

Although primal man sought to render his world as secure and orderly as was possible, his search for control did not destroy his sense of wonder. The world remained a holy place, charged with mystery which could only be approached with reverence. Perhaps the key to the retention of the sense of wonder lies in the avoidance of the attitude of pride (*hubris*). Primal man sought control over the world in the spirit of cooperation rather than exploitation. He experienced his ability to control with a sense of gratitude and not as a right to control (which, when thwarted, gives rise to resentment). This might remain as the summary achievement of primal man: in a fickle world he acted with wonder, and although visited by fear and anxiety, he nevertheless managed to retain his sense of gratitude and to avoid that basic sense of mistrust and resentment which poisons the springs of life.

2. GREEK MAN—REASON AND WONDER

In passing from primal to Greek man, we move from a world view which was expressed in mythical terms to one which was largely articulated in conceptual, philosophical categories. The rich imagery of the gods and Mother Earth was gradually replaced by language about reason (*logos*), ideals or archetypes, and a divine cosmos. However, we must not be misled by the difference in language to assume a fundamental difference in world view. As Greek philosophers developed the ideas of cosmic reason and of a teleological universe, they were but telling, in the new idiom of idealistic philosophy, the old story of a universe inhabited by powers that were friendly to the deepest needs of the human spirt.

Greek philosophy arose at a time when the traditional religious mythology was losing its hold over the more educated classes. The stories of the gods had become so vulgar and so transparently anthropomorphic that neither the morally earnest nor the religiously sensitive found them credible. The earliest philosophers sought to demythologize traditional theology and replace it with a new language and a new approach to the holy. The idea of cosmic reason came to replace Olympian theology, philosophy replaced sacrifice and divination as the path to knowledge of the divine, and the philosopher (in particular, the winsome figure of Socrates) became the new model of authentic human life.

It is, therefore, by looking at the philosophical vision and the relationship between reason—the instrument of philosophy—and wonder that we shall see most clearly the fundamental attitudes and values that animated Greek man.

WONDER AND PHILOSOPHY

The centrality of wonder in Greek thought became evident when Plato had Socrates proclaim that it was the source and foundation of philosophy, which was, in turn, the highest human activity. When Theaetetus expressed his amazement, Socrates replied, "I see, my dear Theaetetus, that Theodorus had a true insight into your nature when he said that you were a philosopher, for wonder (*thaumazein*) is the feeling of a philosopher, and philosophy begins in wonder."[11] Aristotle echoed his teacher in regarding wonder as central to philosophy: "It is owing to their wonder that men both now begin and at first began to philosophize."[12]

The reason that Greek philosophy both began and continued in wonder was because the philosopher was at once more ignorant and more learned than the common man; he was both agnostic and gnostic. Wonder, as the fundamental philosophical mood, pointed in two seemingly opposite directions: toward the superior form of ignorance which was necessary if philosophical questions were to arise, and toward the contemplative or theoretical knowledge of universal truths which the philosopher alone attained.

Wonder as Agnosticism

The common man lived in a world of accepted meanings; he was comfortable in the certainties and explanations that were a part of his social milieu and ideological heritage. By contrast, the philosopher found himself ill at ease in the world and, in moods of amazement, puzzlement, and curiosity, found himself questioning commonly accepted meanings and explanations. As Aristotle characterized philosophers,

They wondered originally at the obvious difficulties, then advanced little by little and stated difficulties about the greater matters, e.g., about the phenomena of the moon and those of the sun and of the stars, and about the genesis of the universe. And a man who is puzzled and wonders thinks himself ignorant (whence even the lover of myth is in a sense a lover of Wisdom, for the myth is composed of wonders); therefore since they philosophized in order to escape from ignorance, evidently they were pursuing science in order to know, and not for any utilitarian end.[13]

There is no better place to see wonder as philosophical ignorance exemplified than in Socrates, whose life and death were as central to subsequent Greek thinking as Christ's was to Christian thought. The superiority of Socrates was in his strange combination of ignorance and certainty. During his life he constantly questioned the values and opinions blindly accepted by most of his contemporaries; yet in facing death he seemed confident of immortality and evidenced a moral courage characteristic only of those who are certain of their values. According to tradition, the oracle at Delphi reported that Socrates was the wisest of all Greeks. This so startled Socrates that he concluded that his superiority in wisdom could only lie in his certainty that he did not know what others pretended to know. Out of this learned ignorance he developed a method of investigating by questioning which profoundly disturbed those who were secure in their assumed knowledge.

A typical example is found in the early dialogue *Euthyphro.* Euthyphro was certain that he understood the nature of piety, and he undertook to instruct Socrates. By the end of the dialogue, however, he had been infected with some of the ignorance of Socrates (or perhaps merely with confusion), while Socrates began to look anew for the essence of piety.

The philosopher, then, lived in amazement and questioning and was never able to domesticate the world in the manner of ordinary men. Questioning and searching for knowledge were for him a continuing way of life. Philosophy was not the achievement of wisdom but the perpetual quest for it; therefore wonder was an abiding attitude in the philosophical life and was never, like curiosity, alleviated by an explanation.[14]

Contemplative or Theoretical Wonder

As we have noted, wonder issued not only in philosophical ignorance but in a superior form of contemplative or theoretical knowledge. Out of ignorance grew questioning (the dialectical method), and questioning led to the threshold of true knowledge. In the famous analogy of the cave in the *Republic,* as well as in the *Symposium,* Plato showed us how philosophy led from shadows to realities, from opinion to knowledge, from a confused awareness of particulars to a clear intuitive knowledge of universals, from mere instances to archetypes. The mind worked its way up the hierarchy of reality by the use of dialectic. Beginning from individual examples of beauty, for instance, in the world of sense,

. . . and using them as steps to ascend continually with that absolute beauty as one's aim, from one instance of physical beauty to two and from two to all, then from physical beauty to moral beauty, and from moral beauty to beauty of knowledge, until from knowledge of various kinds one arrives at the supreme knowledge whose sole object is that absolute beauty.[15]

When the mind reached the highest point in knowledge of the universals, whether of beauty, truth, or goodness, it ceased to reason discursively, ceased the intellectual labor of dialectic, and was lost in leisurely contemplation of the absolute. In contemplation the highest form of universal knowledge was *given* to the philosopher. In a state of relaxed receptivity, in intuition which happened in the presence of the universals, the mind received its highest form of knowledge—the revelation of ultimate principles which were the foundation of the beauty, order, and unity seen in the cosmos. This highest form of knowledge, which involved intellectual vision, was called contemplation, speculation, or theoretical knowledge. To speculate, for the Greek mind, was not to make wild guesses but to look at; to be theoretical was indeed not to hide in a cloud of abstractions but to receive the knowledge of reality into oneself as a gift by intellectual intuition. Hannah Arendt has suggested that *"Theoria,* in fact, is only another word for *thaumazein;* the contemplation of truth at which the philosopher ultimately arrives is the philosophically purified speechless wonder with which he began."[16] *Contemplative & theoretical*

Thus, philosophy both began and ended in wonder. In the be-*puzzles* ginning was the shock of realizing that the cosmos existed when it need not have. Under the impulse of this shock the mind began its journey in quest of an explanation. When, finally, dialectic carried the philosophical consciousness near the heights of universal knowledge, the laboring intellect fell silent and received intuitively, in contemplation, the final vision of that which was the source of all order and intelligibility—what Plato variously called the idea of the Good, Unity, Beauty, or Truth.

In seeing philosophy as an amalgam of wonder and dialectic, Plato combined the Dionysian and Apollonian strands in Greek thought. In wonder there was the Dionysian ecstasy of being possessed by the highest and most divine knowledge. In dialectics there was the Apollonian discipline of intellectual labor which sought to measure, define, and assign limits to ideas.

Cosmological Wonder   *Why I am*

Besides theoretical wonder, which was the highest form of philosophical knowledge, there was a more common form—cosmological wonder. Contemplation was not limited to the highest mystical vision of absolute principles but was also brought to bear on the divine reason which was obvious, to the Greek mind, in the cosmos. If one were to ask any Greek thinker what evidence he could offer to support the view that universal values were built into the heart of reality—that the cosmos was a teleological system governed by a divine reasoning mind—he would have answered by pointing to the orderliness of nature. For a fundamental axiom of the Greek mind was: where there is order there is mind or reason. In the regular movements of the stars and in the recurring cycle of the seasons there was evidence of a mind operating to bring order out of dis-order, to create a cosmos out of chaos. The world was a uni-verse, a rational totality in which day followed night, horses gave birth to horses, and orange trees strangely continued to produce oranges and not tigers hanging by their tails. The cosmos was the incarnation of the ideals of a reasoning mind; it was the arena in which divine reason was actively triumphing over the chaos of disorder, contingency, and chance.

Since the cosmos showed evidence of the incarnation of divine reason, man had to orient himself to his world by contemplating the meaning and order implicit within it before he could act in any appropriate fashion. Wisdom began by looking, not by acting (as in the pragmatic philosophy of modern man). Contemplation of the gift of value which was homogenized into the world must be prior to authentic human action. Hannah Arendt has noted that for the Greek mind,

The primacy of contemplation over activity rests on the conviction that no work of human hands can equal in beauty and truth the physical kosmos, which swings in itself in changeless eternity without any interference or assistance from outside, from man or god. This eternity discloses itself to mortal eyes only when all human movements and activities are at perfect rest.[17]

As Plato said, "time is the moving image of eternity." Hence, the eternal verities which could be known intuitively or theoretically in the highest reaches of philosophical contemplation also became obvious to the less philosophical eye when it turned in wonder to gaze upon the cosmos.

WONDER, FABRICATION, AND ACTION

Contemplation, or philosophical wonder, was the most revered human attitude not only because of the intrinsic value of theoretical vision of the ultimate ideals and the divine order of the cosmos, but because theory preceded practice and receptivity preceded activity. All authentic human fabrication and action were rooted in an awareness of eternal archetypes and patterns of rational order. Before man could make or do, he had to look; human creativity began with a reverence for the divine patterns of meaning and order that were already given.

Perhaps the clearest example of the integral relation between philosophical wonder, fabrication, and action is found in the *Republic,* where Plato proposed that philosophers be the rulers of the ideal state because they alone had a clear vision of the heavenly pattern of the ideal city. Like good craftsmen who copied their design from an eternal model, the philosopher-kings would seek to make the human state as close to the ideal as possible. A city whose blueprint was not conceived in ecstasy would be unstable. A philosopher who was unacquainted with Dionysus was unfit to undertake the political task of shaping the republic.

This basic relation between contemplation and fabrication was carried over also into Plato's cosmology. In the *Timaeus* Plato made clear that even the Demiurge (the architect god who was the symbol for all the rational forces operating in the cosmos to bring order out of disorder) did not create the patterns of meaning *ex nihilo* but, rather, "looked" to a preexisting eternal model of what a cosmos should be. Unlike the Judeo-Christian creation story, the Platonic account insisted that the creator-god was limited by having to accept both the recalcitrance of chaotic "matter" and a preexistent "blueprint" of the ideals which were to be molded into the cosmos. Neither the Demiurge nor the human craftsman was able to fabricate a product which reproduced the perfection of the ideal; however, the Demiurge, being good, did the best job possible, given the limitations. In a like fashion the authentic human actor must look to the eternal ideals, which could be known through discursive reason and wondering contemplation, and seek to impregnate his society and his personal life with rational order.

CONTINUITY BETWEEN PRIMAL AND GREEK MAN

In conclusion, we may note the essential continuity between the Greek world view, especially as it was articulated in Plato, and that of primal man. Primal man constructed his village and his life on patterns which were revealed by the gods. The authentic life was lived in the spirit of cooperation with the powers responsible for the succoring order of nature. In similar fashion, the Greek tradition saw divine rationality operating both in the cosmos and in the *polis* and demanded of man that he apply the law of reason to those unruly passions which threatened to disrupt personality and society. In becoming reasonable, man was a vicegerent of that divine rationality which was at work in all things; he cooperated with cosmic reason. Thus, humility was the precondition of authentic human life. The effort to control the sometimes chaotic environment, to act and manipulate nature, was clearly sanctioned both by primal man and by Greek man. Authentic action arose only in a wondering sensitivity to the forces apart from man which were already operative in the cosmos to maximize order and value. Such awareness was reverence; it was the opposite of pride *(hubris)*, which assumed that human freedom was unlimited and could fabricate its world of meaning *ex nihilo*.

Another element which marks the continuity between primal and Greek man is the seemingly different notions of a world-pole and of human reason as *logos*. Primal man organized his life around a center point (which Eliade has called a world-pole) where the nature of the sacred was revealed. He built his house, his village, and his temple as models of the cosmos; he cosmocized himself. Likewise, Greek man organized his life in conformity with patterns which he found in the cosmos. Human reason was cosmological; it reflected the structure of the whole. Man was a microcosm, a being capable, through wonder and discursive thought, of grasping the principles upon which the cosmos was structured and of giving his life a comparable order.

Before turning to the Judeo-Christian world, one characteristic of both primal and Greek understandings of wonder must be made explicit. Wonder was a pervasive phenomenon appropriate at any point of man's experience of the world. It might equally well be considered under sociology, theology, psychology, cosmology, physics, or agriculture. The significance of this can hardly be overemphasized. *For primal and Greek man, the holy could be encountered at any point; it was revealed primarily in the ordinary experiences of life rather than in the extraordinary.* The philosopher, wondering at the cosmos, could see that divine reason was present wherever order prevailed over disorder and reason over contingency. The common man could express this same conviction of the universal presence of the holy by speaking of the sea as Poseidon, of love as Aphrodite, of Athena as the goddess and protector of the polis, or of Artemis as goddess of wild things. The sacrament of communion with the holy might take place in any grove or assembly; the triumph of reason over contingency could be celebrated any time man gave himself over to wonder and action.

3. JUDEO-CHRISTIAN MAN—REVELATION, CREATION, AND WONDER

When we pass from the Greek tradition to a consideration of the Judeo-Christian world view, intellectual fashion seems to dictate that we abandon the continuity motif and speak of discontinuity. A standard item in courses in the history of philosophy and religious thought is the following schema:

Greek Thought	*Hebrew-Christian Thought*
Centered in experience of nature	Centered in the experience of history
Philosophical	Theological
Anthropocentric or cosmocentric	Theocentric
Reason is the essence of man.	Being addressed by God and responding in faith is the essence of man.
Abstract, universal, conceptual patterns of thought are dominant. Thought aims at attaining static, nonhistorical, metaphysical truths.	Concrete, particular, dramatic patterns of thought are dominant. Thought aims at grasping dynamic, historical realities.
Religion of Greeks is man's ladder of ascent to God.	Revelation in the Judeo-Christian tradition is God's condescending to man.
The highest form of love is *eros*, which is love recognizing value in its object.	*Agape* is the highest form of love, a self-giving form of love.
Rooted in attitudes of ontological, theoretical, and cosmological wonder.	Rooted in historical wonders

Without doubt, there is a measure of truth in such a schema. However, it so emphasizes differences that the more important similarities are overlooked. The squabble between Athens and Jerusalem is a family affair! Primal man, Greek man, and Judeo-Christian man are but three species within a single genus which may be called *homo admirans* (wondering man), teleological man, or idealistic man. They share the assumption that the cosmos is a teleologically ordered system, governed by a rational mind or minds comprehensible to the human mind. Their major differences concern the questions of whether the mind ordering the cosmos is immanent or transcendent and whether evidence for this mind is found primarily in the recurring sequences of nature or in the unique events of human history. As we shall see in a later chapter, the irreconcilable conflict is not between the primal-Greek and the Hebrew-Christian views of man but between the traditional notion that man lives in wonder in a cosmos already partially informed by patterns of meaning and value, and the modern view that man lives in constant anxiety in a chaos which he alone must shape and make meaningful.

REVELATION AS WONDER-EVENT—THE BIRTH OF HISTORICAL WONDER

The organizing center for both Hebrew and Christian thought is made up of certain unique events which the respective communities hold to be revelations of God's will and purpose for His people. The central events are the Exodus, the giving of the law, and the life, death, and resurrection of Jesus. Although Hebrew and Christian views are not in complete agreement about which events are revelatory, they do agree in maintaining, contrary to both primal and Greek views, that the Holy Mind responsible for the cosmos is known primarily in the unrepeatable events of history rather than in the orderly cycle of nature. God is not homogenized into the cosmic process but is its transcendent creator; therefore He may be known only by inference from the process. He is more directly known only where He has chosen to make special revelations. This eventual and historical character of Hebrew-Christian thought has been sufficiently explored in recent literature and needs no further elaboration.

What must be emphasized here is the creation of a new type of wonder: historical wonder. The crucial events in the Biblical tradition testifying to the revelation of God in history are called marvels, signs, or wonders. A revelatory event is a wonder-event. Since the character of revelation is occasional rather than perpetual, it is with wonders rather than the wonder of the cosmos that the Biblical tradition is primarily concerned. Historical wonder, rather than ontological wonder, characterizes the Biblical tradition.

If we are to understand the part wonder plays in the Hebrew-Christian tradition, we must go beyond the central category of revelation as a wonder-event and examine the way in which the Biblical understanding of man served to recommend that whole range of attitudes which we have earlier found to be associated with wonder. In order to do this we will concentrate upon one doctrine held in common by Judaism and Christianity: the doctrine of creation. Our analysis will distinguish between the implicit significance of the doctrine of creation and its historical significance.

CREATION AND WONDER

Creation as Gift

A discussion of the fundamental world view of the Judeo-Christian tradition must begin with creation. Although neither Greek nor Hebrew thought attributed creation to the gods or God until late in their development, we are currently in the West established in a form of religious experience and thought in which God is seen, first of all, as creator.

The language of creation, whether in the *Timaeus* or Genesis or popular religious thought, begins at the beginning of time: "In the beginning God created the heavens and the earth." Creation is a once-upon-a-time story as it is first told. However, theological reflection quickly qualifies the temporal language and makes it serve as an ontological statement. In the *Timaeus,* for instance, the creation story is obviously Plato's way of giving an analysis of the basic principles which are necessary to explain the nature of the currently actual state of affairs. Both Jewish and Christian theologians likewise have made clear that creation is not merely a past act but is the action of God in every mode of time. God has created, does create, and will create. Thus, the language of creation is not primarily a way of settling the problem of origins but is a way of making a statement about the source and foundation of life.

To speak of creation is at once to reject the negative interpretation of life as an accident and to make the positive affirmation that life is a gift. In the Judeo-Christian tradition the creating God not only pronounces His work good but reveals Himself as one who cares for and succors His creatures. Historically, the conviction that God cares for His chosen people predates the idea that He is the creator of the universe; the children of Israel confess that God brought them up out of Egypt before they claim that Yahweh was the creator of all. Thus, when the theology of creation arises, it is already informed by a theology of salvation. The one who creates is Father, and His motivation in giving life is love. In the *Timaeus* as well, although it is not a myth of creation *ex nihilo,* Plato takes care to point out that the motivation of the power that shapes the universe is benevolent. "Let us, then, state for what reason becoming and this universe were framed by him who framed them. He was good; and in the good no jealousy in any matter can ever arise. So, being without jealousy, he desired that all things should come as near as possible to being like himself."[18]

There can be no question of the fact that the doctrine of creation has frequently functioned both in Judaism and in Christianity within the context of a legalistic view of the relationship between God and man. When this mood has dominated, the gift of life granted in creation has been seen to be a loan or a debt that must be repaid—indeed, no gift at all. God has given us life; hence, we are His possessions and "owe" Him obedience. This juristic and legalistic view can only be combated if creation is understood as a free and generous gift. This requires that we strike a careful balance between two ideas—the notion that man is a creature and the notion that he is created in the image of God. The meaning of creation as a gift depends upon these fundamental Biblical notions.

Man as Creature

To affirm that man is a creature signifies that life is a gift, having structure, meaning, and built-in limits. According to the Biblical tradition, man is *something*—he is not *everything;* he does not make himself but comes into a world already richly informed with psychological, biological, physical, and sociological patterns of meaning. We are, as Merleau-Ponty said, "condemned to meaning." However plastic the ingenuity of man may make the limits of life, there are limiting conditions that he cannot transcend. We are born either male or female, with the necessity to sleep, eat, work, love, talk together, and discover the meaning of human existence. The categories of our minds and the cells of our bodies are molded by belonging to time and space, and finally all our days are shaped by the fact that eventually we reach that most terrifying of all limits—death. In affirming that man is a creature and that creaturely life is a gift, the Biblical tradition is proclaiming that in spite of finitude, evil, and death, life is nevertheless good. Man need not be immortal or omnipotent for his life to be viewed as a gift.

Thus, the doctrine of the creatureliness of man implies the negation of that all-or-nothing attitude which would deny the designation "gift" to any form of life which has limits. Nietzsche's expression of this attitude is graphic: "If there were gods, how could I endure not to be a god! Hence there are no gods."[19] The doctrine of creation answers Nietzsche's question, if it is a question and not a mere cry of rebellion, with the recognition that the gift of life is inseparable from its limits. Precisely because human life is finite, it can be considered a gift. The conditions under which life is given are not evidence that the creator of life harbors the hidden intent of enslaving and possessing man and placing him under the horrible burden of a sense of total obligation. Human freedom is not destroyed by acknowledging that it has limits; it is merely understood as *human freedom*. Acknowledging limits is the same as acknowledging the definite shape of that gift which is human life. This is no more repressive of freedom or destructive of dignity than the insistence of a psychiatrist that his patient will live a more rewarding life if he abandons his omnipotent claims to power, freedom, and creativity, and instead invests his imagination and energy in being creative within realistic limts. To be something definite is to have limits.

Man as Image of God

Balancing the doctrine of the creatureliness of man is the idea that he is created in the image of God. Although the notion of the image of God plays only a small part in Biblical theology, it assumed a central place in traditional Jewish and Christian thought. That man is created in the image of God means that he is given lordship over the earth. Within the limits of the givenness of finite existence, man gives structure and meaning to his world. Man is a creator of meaning and value. As a creature, he must discover and accept the meaning implicit in the world into which he emerges, but as one created in the image of God, man is a creator of meaning. Thus, man's creative potential is real but not unlimited; it is his responsibility to complete the creation of a world that has been turned over to him only partially informed with meaning. Within the range of what is humanly possible, it is his responsibility to experiment and to create ever richer patterns of meaning and relationship. The humanization of earth is the task of the creature; hence, the doctrine of the image of God should be an impetus to destroy all those forms of psychological and social organization which are repressive and destructive of human dignity and create those forms in which human potentiality can be fulfilled. If we ask, in light of the doctrine of creation, to what extent man is responsible for creating a meaningful world, the answer can only be: almost totally. Grace is the gift of responsible freedom. The dignity of human life lies in its ability to decide, to act, and to create. One might say that, from a Judeo-Christian perspective, Sartre is almost right—human freedom is practically unlimited. The only limiting factor is the givenness of life, which may be perceived either as grace or as an absurd datum.

Creation and Situated Existence

Thus far I have spoken of creation as an affirmation in general terms that the universe is a gift and not an accident. We must recognize, however, that the doctrine of creation functions on a much more existential and intimate level in the life of the believer. Not human existence in general but *my* life is the functional focal point of the doctrine of creation. As I experience my life, it seems initially as if all the events that conspired to create me as a unique individual are purely accidental. Is it not pure chance that accounts for the formative influence of my parents, the religion in which I was raised, the girl I married, the profession I entered, and the level of physical and psychological health which is inseparable from my outlook on life? And yet, if all these formative events are chance-governed, does it make any sense for me to affirm that the cosmos and human existence in general are gifts mediating the presence of a caring God? Can God be present in the creation of the cosmos and not of the individual?

The doctrine of creation functions to affirm that the seemingly contingent events by which I was formed are also to be accepted under the category of gift. Gabriel Marcel says that to speak of creation is to affirm "the noncontingency of the empirical datum."[20] By this he means that events (such as illness or the meeting on a train with a stranger who later becomes my wife) which appear purely accidental to the objective observer are experienced within faith as an integral and necessary part of the believer's world. The unique shape of my life is to be found in my response to the events that make up my world. This denial that accident and chance are the ultimate categories by which I am to understand the givenness of my life does not imply the extreme affirmation that my life is, therefore, governed by necessity, that it merely involves the unrolling of a preconceived cosmic plan. Freedom is real even if it must operate within the context of some necessity.

To affirm that God is creator signifies functionally that I must exercise a combination of acceptance and responsibility, of discovery and creation of meaning with regard to the given data that compose my personal world. This dual attitude is the precondition of my being able to exploit my individual potentialities. To refuse to acknowledge that I must discover meaning is to deny that my destiny is shaped by incarnation in a body and a historical situation; to refuse to accept responsibility for creating meaning is to deny my ability to transcend the givenness of my life.

Attitudinal Responses

We may conclude our discussion of creation by noting some of the attitudes and dispositions to action which are appropriate responses to the symbolic affirmation that life is a gift from a creator.

If the doctrine of creation signifies that life is to be perceived as a gift, the appropriate response to this perception will be thankfulness and celebration. *Life is to be lived under the sign of gratitude and not obligation; it is not a debt to be repaid but a gift to be enjoyed.* Thus, to say that man is a creature is to make inappropriate the overwhelming sense of oughtness and the consequent guilt, resentment, and nay-saying which, as Nietzsche noted, frequently accompany belief in God.

Expectancy, openness to novelty, and astonishment make up the second cluster of attitudes which are appropriate in a created order. Since creation refers to all three modes of time, every present moment is contained within "the eighth day of creation." Novelty is always possible, since life is not the vain repetition of preprogramed laws of a mechanical system but the creative interplay of the divine ground and finite freedom. Expectancy regarding the present and the future precludes that attitude which is the most deadly enemy of wonder—boredom. Boredom is inevitable when history may bring forth no new possibilities; when the future is closed, the present becomes a time of despair. Ecclesiastes, caught in the fatalism of the decaying Greek cyclical view of history, expresses well the deadly inevitability that governs history when novelty is no longer possible.

All things are full of weariness: a man cannot utter it; the eye is not satisfied with seeing, nor the ear filled with hearing. What has been is what will be, and what has been done is what will be done; and there is nothing new under the sun. Is there a thing of which it is said, "See, this is new?" It has been already, in the ages before us.[21]

Eliot expresses this same sense of tedium:

> For I have known them all already, known them all;
> Have known the evenings, mornings, afternoons,
> I have measured out my life with coffee spoons.[22]

The doctrine of creation, by affirming that the present and the future are in the ultimate category of gift and not chance or necessity, makes appropriate that astonishment which is historical wonder and that expectancy toward the future which is hope.

So much for the view of the world and human existence which is contained *in principle* in the Judeo-Christian affirmation of creation. In the messiness of history, principle and fact seldom coincide. It is as Eliot has reminded us—between the idea and the reality falls the shadow. In the history of Western religious thought and institutions the richness of meaning implicit in the doctrine of creation was very imperfectly translated into action. To absorb the implications of the doctrine of creation into the substance of life is to be animated by the spirit of gratitude, expectancy, trust, and wonder, and therefore to live in continuity with primal and Greek man. However, certain unresolved tensions within Judeo-Christian theology and religious institutions have contributed to the nullification of those very attitudes which the doctrine of creation intends, and have contributed to the eclipse of wonder.

TENSIONS WITHIN JUDEO-CHRISTIAN THEOLOGY

The doctrines of creation and the logos provided the requisite theological principles for integrating cosmological and historical wonder, thus making it possible to experience the holy in any event or place. The theological framework was present to duplicate the possibility that existed for primal and Greek man of encountering the holy equally in the ordinary or the extraordinary experiences of life, and thus of proclaiming all of man's life, not merely one aspect of it, sacred. While the doctrine of creation might have led to a sacramental view of all of life, it did not. The divorce between wonder and the holy which has taken place in Western civilization can be traced, in some measure, to the unresolved tensions in the Judeo-Christian views of creation and redemption. In choosing as organizing principles wonder-events which were unique and unrepeatable as the sphere of God's self-revelation, both Judaism and Christianity created communities which preserved the memory of the crucial events; thus, a tension was created between

The wonder-event which is the foundation of the unique community that recollects it.	[and]	The wonder of human existence in the heart of nature and the cosmos which is a fundamental experience of the universal community of man.
Sacred history		Secular, universal history
The Hebrew-Christian institutions		The Gentile-pagan world
Grace and faith		Nature and reason
Historical wonder before the Exodus, the Incarnation, etc.		Ontological wonder before the givenness of being

The tension between the two types of experience represented in this polarity is not, in theory, destructive. Tension need not lead to dichotomy. However, a dichotomy in fact developed in Western self-understanding, a kind of practical gnosticism or functional dualism. God became imprisoned in ecclesiastical language and structures, in the thought forms, institutions, and history of a single people, in special experiences labeled "religious." A dualism developed between the Wholly Other God—whose sanctifying presence was definitively known in His revelation in the Hebrew-Christian tradition—and the secular world, which was filled with much that was meaningful and valuable but was no longer considered a medium of revelation. A gulf opened between the holy and the wonder-ful.

This dichotomy, or practical gnosticism, can best be seen in the relationship which has existed between the Christian Church and nature. In affirming that God is not to be known definitively in the natural course of events but in special wonder-events, Christian theology accomplished a desacralization of nature, a destruction of the presence of the holy at the heart of the everyday. As D. H. Lawrence so vividly expressed it, "Christ killed the great god Pan." Harvey Cox has tried to make a virtue out of necessity and has proclaimed that this very desacralization of nature provided the necessary neutral sphere within which natural science and empirical investigation could arise; hence the Hebrew-Christian view of creation is credited with being primarily responsible for the development of Western science and technology. The difficulty with this interpretation is that it is not supported by the facts. The Christian Church has consistently resisted the development of modern science and technology until relatively recently! Galileo, Darwin, and Freud were by no means early candidates for canonization. Man's love affair with the natural order—which arose as much out of reverent curiosity and wonder as out of a desire to control—has been the subject of many ecclesiastical suits for the alienation of affection. Hebrew-Christian orthodoxy has continued to maintain that man's focal point for the discovery of dignity, meaning, and value must be in the special experiences and history which are celebrated in the synagogue and the church. There has been a grudging concession that science, technology, and the empirical temper have created a higher and more comfortable standard of living, but at the same time we are reminded that luxury and variety have nothing to do with salvation. Man may wonder at the mystery of nature and learn to control it creatively, but holiness is still to be found primarily where the language of Israel is spoken—such has been the attitude of the Hebrew-Christian tradition, at least in its popular and most influential manifestations.

This same split is evident in the schizophrenic doctrine of man which is still the basis of popular religious morality. The body and the sensations, which belong to involvement with the natural and material world rather than to history (memory is the organ of history) are religiously suspect. Ask any unsophisticated religious group to free-associate from the word "sin": the immediate response will always be "sex." Sex and the celebration of the senses in art are religiously neutral if not suspect. Wonder, which has also been given to the arts ("Isn't wonder a *merely* aesthetic attitude?"), may enhance our sense of the beautiful, but it still reaches no higher than the sphere of the secular in popular Christian theology. Ontological wonder has to do with sensation, body, and nature, all of which remain in the realm of the profane, while historical wonder, more properly called faith, is the means to the intuition of the holy.

That alteration in Western self-understanding which has lately emerged under the banner of the "death of God" is largely a result of the dichotomy of which I have spoken. When God becomes segregated from the times, spaces, and activities in which the majority of life is lived—when a wedge is driven between the holy and the quotidian—the concept of God becomes either insignificant or positively repressive and must be rejected if the integrity of human life is to be retained. A God who does not sanctify the everyday is dead, and belief in such a remote God is an intellectual or aesthetic luxury which is of no positive consequence, as it does not lead to the celebration of life. An unemployed God quickly exhausts his capital and becomes a dead God. Since man is a totality, faith cannot be separated from reason, spirit from body, history from nature, or the unique from the quotidian without paying the price of schizophrenia. And before man will accept schizophrenia as his permanent condition, he will kill off any god who prevents his reunion with himself. In large measure the story of the eclipse of wonder (which is the same story as the death of God, the loss of the holy, the secularization of Western culture, and the loss of cosmic reason) is the outcome of the unsolved dichotomy between the sacred and the profane which was bequeathed to Western man by the Judeo-Christian tradition. To that story we now turn.

When I consider the short extent of my life, swallowed up in the eternity before and after, the small space that I fill or even see, engulfed in the infinite immensity of spaces unknown to me and which know me not, I am terrified and astounded to find myself here and not there. For there is no reason why it should be here, not there, why now rather than at another time.

—BLAISE PASCAL[1]

Brief and powerless is man's life; on him and all his race the slow, sure doom falls pitiless and dark. Blind to good and evil, reckless of destruction, omnipotent matter rolls on its relentless way; for man, condemned today to lose his dearest, tomorow himself to pass through the gate of darkness, it remains only to cherish, ere yet the blow fall, the lofty thoughts that ennoble his little day; disdaining the coward terrors of the slave of Fate, to worship at the shrine that his own hands have built; undismayed by the empire of chance, to preserve a mind free from the wanton tyranny that rules his outward life; proudly defiant of the irresistible forces that tolerate, for a moment, his knowledge and his condemnation, to sustain, alone, a weary but unyielding Atlas, the world that his own ideals have fashioned despite the trampling march of unconscious power.

—BERTRAND RUSSELL[2]

Every existing thing is born without reason, prolongs itself out of weakness and dies by chance.

—JEAN PAUL SARTRE[3]

CHAPTER IV

The Chaotic World
of Modern Man

Having seen the unity underlying seemingly different modes of self-understanding of traditional man, we now take a giant step to modern man without any attempt to trace the exact route by which we arrived at our present condition. The notion of "modern man" is no less a philosophical construct than that of "traditional man." In actuality there was much technological and empirical thought among tribal peoples, just as there is much magical thought in contemporary life. Even in the highly secularized West perhaps a majority still confess some form of religious faith. In speaking of modern man I wish to characterize a type of self-and-world-understanding that is increasingly coming to dominate Western thought as it is articulated by the most influential novelists, artists, and philosophers of our time. Whether the self-understanding of what we are calling modern man can claim a statistical majority in contemporary Western culture is both difficult and unnecessary to determine. My purpose here is to take what is certainly a significant way of understanding man, which lays claim to being modern, and contrast it with the consensus we found to be operative in traditional self-understanding.

Our focus in this chapter will be on the destruction of *the ecology of wonder*. An attitude as fundamental as wonder can exist only so long as there is a philosophical context which makes it an appropriate way of feeling about the world. Any fundamental feeling-response must be supported by a world view or else it becomes an antique emotion. Our task here is to look at the way modern man views his world, to discover whether it remains appropriate to wonder. We shall find, in this chapter and the next, that only a truncated form of wonder can survive in the caustic spiritual environment which modern man has created for himself. Wonder may survive as a quaint feeling or as sentimentality, but not as a revelatory emotion.

Our method of dealing with modern man will be to make a somewhat arbitrary division between ways of looking at the world and models of self-understanding. In the present chapter we shall explore the way modern man looks at the context of his existence, and in the following chapter we shall see how he understands himself in the light of the world he discovers and creates. The first story I have to tell might be called the birth of nihilism and the eclipse of wonder.

I. THE DECLINE OF REASON

FROM COSMIC TO TECHNICAL REASON

The idealistic vision of a reasonably ordered cosmos which traditional man affirmed in his myths, philosophy, and theology grows increasingly dimmer as the twentieth century progresses. Scarcely a trace of it is to be found in contemporary novelists, artists, philosophers, or political thinkers. In the broad community of educated men the conviction that life is to be ordered in conformity with principles which also operate in the objective world has all but ceased to undergird activity and aspiration. As Horkheimer has said, "Reason as an organ for perceiving of our lives has come to be regarded as obsolete. Speculation is synonymous with metaphysics, and metaphysics with mythology and superstition."[4]

The word "reason" has changed its meaning so radically in the twentieth century as to scarcely resemble the idealistic concept. What was once an activity and structure common to man and nonhuman reality has now become the ability to manipulate abstractions and solve problems. Paul Tillich speaks of a change from ontological to technical reason, and Horkheimer speaks of a switch from an objective to a subjective or formalistic concept of reason. We might equally well speak of a shift in the concept of reason from idealistic to empirical, total to formal, metaphysical to scientific, and cosmic to technical. The terminology we use is not so important as the recognition that there is almost unanimous agreement among modern thinkers that man's ability to know, to understand, and to think in an orderly and convincing fashion about the whole context and significance of his life is far more modest and limited than past generations of idealistic thinkers have led us to suppose.

Reason for the most part, in the contemporary understanding, is the ability of the human mind to grasp, manipulate, and seek out necessary connections between ideas. The model of the new concept of reason is mathematics and formal logic, in which absolute certainty may be achieved because there is no distinction between form and content and because no questions of ends or purposes enter in. In a somewhat less rigorous sense, the methodology of the natural sciences is considered reasonable, although certain subjective factors enter into both the formulations of hypotheses and the weighing of evidence. In both of these cases reason has to do with the manipulation of abstractions which are designed to accomplish certain operations. It is a pragmatic activity, issuing in absolute certainty or a high degree of probability.

Perhaps the most articulate defense of this technical view of reason is found in A. J. Ayer's classic statement of positivism, *Language, Truth and Logic.* Ayer argues that the only cognitively meaningful statements are ones which are either true by definition —i.e., analytically true—or empirically verifiable. Metaphysical, moral, and theological statements fall into the category of emotive and cognitively meaningless utterances. This is not to say that they are psychologically meaningless. It is often psychologically meaningful to utter linguistic nonsense—for instance, when we play with children or stammer with grief. Ayer's thesis is important not because it shows philosophical balance and wisdom but because he proclaims with vigor a view of reason which is increasingly dominant in our culture. Reason is scientific abstraction dealing with either formal symbols created by the mind or empirical data.

The technical view of reason excludes from rational discussion most of the questions that philosophy traditionally considered. All metaphysical or metaempirical matters—such as consideration of the value of human life, the nature of good and evil or beauty and beatitude—lie forever in exile in the never-never land of the emotions beyond the pale of verification and cognitive respectability. Kant said there were three questions which reason must answer: What can I know? What ought I to do? What may I hope? Technical reason can approach only the first of these. We can know only the verifiable and the tautological. Questions about the ultimate meaning of human existence and the conduct of life must be handed over to the will and the emotions. Reason meanwhile, back at the laboratory, works away at the "practical" problems of the day, creating at once nuclear monsters which threaten all life and wonderful pills for the prevention of anxiety and for the replacement of what an earlier age called hope. Huxley characterized the situation well in *Ape and Essence* by saying that in a society dominated by technical reason, only the ends are ape-chosen—the means are human.

THE HISTORICITY OF REASON

There is another way in which we might characterize the change reason has undergone. The essence of the traditional, idealistic concept of cosmic reason was the conviction that *history was pervaded (Greek) or had been invaded (Christian) by reason.* The flux, disunity, seeming absurdity, and tragedy that appeared to dominate history and nature were ultimately to yield to the dominion of reason. The current understanding of reason reverses this conviction and asserts that *reason has been invaded by history.* It denies that the categories of human reason are eternal or even transcultural. They are born out of and bound to a specific environment and history. When, for instance, we discover that Buddhist logic differs in its basic categories from Western logic or that concepts of basic morality differ from culture to culture, the conviction grows that reason is relative. Relativism and pluralism are axioms of the modern mind no less than the idealistic conviction was axiomatic for the classical Western mind. To say that man is totally a product of his history and environment is equivalent to saying that there is no human reason in the idealistic sense. For the idealist tradition it was human reason that allowed man to transcend his biased national history and the idiosyncrasies of his biography and communicate both with a nonhistorical Absolute (God or Reason) and with men who did not share a common history.

The conviction that reason is relative has a long history, although it has only recently become an axiom of mass thought. Hume and Kant took the first steps toward the destruction of the cosmic concept of reason in showing that the mind creates rather than discovers the order in nature. This did not lead to relativism, however, because Kant still held that the categories the mind made use of in understanding the world were common to all men and were not generated by any specific environment. Darwin, by implication at least, went a step further in showing that reason itself was a product of nature. Mind evolved from nature before it created history and culture. Even more destructive of the idealistic concept of reason were the theories and discoveries of Marx and Freud. Marx held that many of our most treasured ideas, supposedly discovered by reason, were in fact ideologies, conceptual weapons in the struggle for economic domination. Freud further dispelled the illusion of the rational man. Man, he said, was dominated by irrational forces, subject to unconscious motivation, and frequently substituted rationalization for reason. Perhaps even more important than specific philosophical ideas in creating a widespread distrust of reason and a belief in relativism has been the influence of modern advertising and propaganda techniques and mass communication. The ethical and cultural relativism which was once an element only in the thought of anthropologists world travelers, and intellectuals now seems an almost inevitable conclusion to every television watcher. The ubiquity of propaganda aimed at selling a product or a government policy has further destroyed the confidence in reason. The word is no longer bound to *logos* but to manipulation; the connection between word, reason, and truth which was at the heart of the idealistic concept of reason is destroyed when words are used solely to induce a hearer to conform to the desires of the speaker.

2. THE NEW MULTIVERSE—FROM NECESSITY
TO CONTINGENCY

With the decline of the idealistic concept of reason has gone a related shift in the understanding of the context, or ecology, of human existence. Reason is now exiled in the mind of man, and the world is reasonless. If there is harmony, order, and purpose, it is in the human mind and not in external reality. Modern man thus lives, not in a cosmos but in a chaos, not in a universe but in a multiverse, not in a harmonious whole but in a cacophonous collection of parts. Pluralism, which is so obviously a part of our culture in politics and religion, is also characteristic of the metaphysical situation of modern man. We have returned to a type of demythologized polytheism in which different principles, rules, moral codes, and aims govern different areas of life, and no overarching vision or purpose binds them all together. Politics, worship, business, and personal relations are conducted according to different, and often unrelated, principles. The philosophers of language have recently reminded us that each human activity has its own "language game" and that we risk intellectual and moral confusion when we refuse to recognize the limits of a given game. We dare not, for instance, ask whether the existence of God (theological language game) is verifiable (scientific language game) or whether it is "right" or "good" (ethics) to break treaties which have become politically disadvantageous. For the idealistic tradition, the context of human life was a cosmos precisely because existing "language games" were united by common principles. Metaphysics, theology, politics, personal ethics, and aesthetics had common foundations.

The modern understanding of the world is most adequately summed up in the word "contingent." A contingent event (in the modern meaning of this word) is one which may or may not come to pass, one which is accidental, fortuitous, or depends on chance. The opposite of contingent is rational or necessary.

Within the idealistic world view of traditional man, the existence of man and the events of human history were not contingent or governed merely by chance. Certainly there were chance happen-

IMPORTANT

ings, for not everything down to the slightest detail was determined by Reason, but chance was contained within the context of a meaningful and rationally explainable totality. Chance, like evil, existed, but it was domesticated and kept within bounds by Reason. Thus, in the broadest sense, the world was governed by necessity. Divine Reason had ordained things to serve a purpose in the overall economy of the cosmos, and hence there was a rational necessity for things to be as they were were. If things were not always as they should be to fulfill the demands of reason and the desires of the heart, it was because something, for the time being, resisted being incorporated into the design of Reason (for Plato, erratic motion, and for Christians, the Devil).

It was David Hume (1711–1776) who first made a decisive philosophical attack on the idea of necessity. Necessity, he showed, belonged not to the actual world but only to the inner world of ideas. So long as we remain within the mental kingdom of the syllogism, we can be certain, for instance, that Socrates will be forever mortal, since it follows logically and necessarily from the major and minor premises (all men are mortal; Socrates is a man). But once we step outside the mental world into the real world, logical necessity gives way to mere psychological certainty. We are reasonably certain that every man is mortal, that the sun will rise tomorrow, or that apple trees will continue to bear apples and not oranges, but an exception is possible. We can conceive of an immortal man, a sunless day, or nuts growing on an apple tree. Although no one of these exceptions is likely, it is not impossible. Where a logical necessity binds ideas together, we cannot even imagine any other possibility than the inevitable one. We cannot imagine two plus two not equaling four or a bachelor who would be married, because there is a necessary and logical connection between the ideas. Bachelors are forbidden by logic to be married.

The importance of this distinction made by Hume is enormous. It is hardly too much to say that modern philosophy was born with the conviction that the laws of reason were to be found within the mind of man and not in the objective world. Someone summed up the impact of Hume's philosophy by saying that for Hume "one damn thing just followed another." There was no reason why events had to follow as they did, for there could never be a necessary connection between any two matters of fact. When we say that one event causes another, the only thing we really mean is that the first event has, in past cases of observation, always preceded the other. A cause is not a reason or an explanation. If I say that the lowering of the temperature below 32 degrees causes the freezing of water, I am not giving an explanation or a reason for the mysterious fact that freezing occurs; I am only formalizing my observation of *what* happens. Reason may tell us what happens but not why. When Hume's insight that contingency and not necessity rules in the real world was absorbed and applied to human life, a new type of philosophy arose—existentialism.

Kierkegaard was the first thinker to see the existential implications of the idea of contingency. While Hume turned from philosophy to backgammon rather than live in the contingent world that his mind had discovered, Kierkegaard chose to live on the edge of despair by the continual repetition of the leap of faith. It was against the idealism of Hegel that Kierkegaard defined his philosophy of existence. He denied that human existence could be incorporated into a rational system or that the contradictions of experience could assume a rational harmony from the human perspective. Possibly, Kierkegaard admitted, from God's point of view reality might be a rational system. But man could experience his existence only from the limited perspective of history, and he made himself ridiculous when he tried, as Hegel had done, to assume the perspective of the Absolute Mind. The tragedy, contradiction, and contingency of history are abiding aspects of human existence, and it is within this situation of limited vision that man must make a decision about the meaning of his existence—a leap of faith, which cannot be justified by reason.

Kierkegaard never pushed the vision of contingency to its logical conclusion, for he was shaped far more than he realized by the idealistic presuppositions of Hegel. He tipped his hand when he tried to give a justification of Christian faith. The Incarnation was, according to his understanding, not rational in any sense but a complete paradox, an event so outrageously contradictory that it could be believed only in spite of human reason. The very passion created by belief in the absurd was the criterion for the truth of faith. Truth, he said, is "an objective uncertainty held fast in an appropriation-process of the most passionate inwardness." The crucial point here is one which Kierkegaard seems to have missed. An event may be paradoxical or absurd, an offense to reason, only if there is another class of events which is not absurd, i.e., a class of reasonable events. Thus, the concept of a paradoxical event has meaning only within a world view which is basically idealistic, one in which a reason may be assigned to normal events but not to paradoxical events.

The full significance of contingency is finally recognized by Sartre and the so-called "atheistic existentialists." With great intellectual vigor and courage Sartre has abandoned the last traces of the idealistic vision of a world ordered by reason and has drawn a portrait of human life in a contingent world. In his novel *Nausea* he describes the experiences of Antoine Roquentin, a writer, who is constantly prey to the experience of metaphysical nausea because he has come to see the world as wholly contingent. Antoine describes his insight in the famous scene in which he is confronted by the chestnut tree, for whose existence he can find no reason.

And without formulating anything clearly, I understood that I had found the key to Existence, the key to my Nauseas, to my own life. In fact, all that I could grasp beyond that returns to this fundamental absurdity. . . . The world of explanations and reasons is not the world of existence. A circle is not absurd. . . . But neither does a circle exist. . . . The essential thing is contingency. I mean that one cannot define existence as necessity. To exist is simply *to be there;* those who exist let themselves be encountered, but you can never deduce anything from them. I believe there are people who have understood this. Only they tried to overcome this contingency by inventing a necessary, causal being. But no necessary being can explain existence; contingency is not a delusion, a probability which can be dissipated; it is the absolute, consequently, the perfect free gift. . . .[5]

The vision of a contingent world introduces a new philosophical situation into Western history. The quest for an explanation of the meaning of human existence in the world has been the driving force in both philosophy and religion in the past. Man has existed in a perennial search for metaphysical identity and meaning. He has continually asked: Who am I? Why are things as they are? For what purpose do I exist? But such questions have no meaning in a contingent world, for no explanations can be given for why things are as they are—only descriptions of what they are. To ask for the ultimate *why* is to ask for a reason, and that is not given in the brute facticity of human existence in the world. Both Heidegger and Sartre tell us that man discovers himself in a world which is devoid of intrinsic rationality. Camus is careful to point out that the essence of the absurdity of the human condition is the contradiction between man's desire for harmony, justice, and reason and the disharmony, injustice, and irrationality of the actual world. This incompatible marriage of desire and fact leads to the proclamation of absurdity.

Both Sartre and Camus present orderly and rationally developed arguments and literary works dedicated to showing that the world is absurd and lacks objective order. Recently a new literature of the absurd has arisen with a form and method appropriate to the message. In the plays of Beckett and Ionesco we are presented with absurdity rather than a reasoned argument about absurdity; we are confronted with dialogue that lacks logical connection, events which bear no relationship to each other, action without consequence, and consequences which happen but are not caused. We are shown a world from which reason has been subtracted, leaving only a series of happenings.

Whether in literature, art, or the theater, the "happening" represents the final triumph of the contingent view of the world. According to Marshal Fishwick, a happening "involves a spontaneous, unrehearsed, and often unconnected cluster of events; a sequence of unstructured and largely unrelated paradoxes that will not resolve dilemmas that will not dissolve. . . . Built on "chance" techniques, happenings relieve everyone of the burden of choosing when to do something."[6]

The happening is a phenomenon which cuts across all the arts in our time; we have choreography by chance, novels with no beginning or end, plays in which audience and actors interact, and artistic "events" in which nothing is produced. If we can believe McLuhan, all of this is characteristic of the new style of perception in which immediate involvement replaces reflective distance. "The instantaneous world of electric informational media involves all of us, all at once. No detachment or frame is possible."[7]

The emerging hero of our time is the antihero, who is able to live in an absurd world with gusto and abandon. As little as a generation ago the heroes of the absurd, such as Roquentin in Sartre's *Nausea* or Dr. Rieux in Camus' *Plague* were striving aggressively to create a moral order in an absurd world. The contemporary absurd hero has abandoned such striving and floats along with whatever happens. The heroes of *Catch 22* or *The Ginger Man,* for instance, have given up making sense out of things —of making history—and consent to accept the absurd without trying to change it.

The world of happenings is of a piece with all the efforts to "blow the mind," with or without drugs. In the absurd world of happenings there are no connections between things; however, thought keeps on trying to make order where none exists. The mind, reason, is a hang-up which creates an artificial world of repressive order. Hence, the absurd hero either stops thinking, like Mersault, or he blows the mind with drugs in order to lose the illusion that there is a connection between mind and reality. Once the mind is blown free of the exigence of reason and the nostalgia for justice and order (which shaped the world of Camus), we can drift in the stream of happenings. The message of the cult of LSD is: Take the anxiety out of contingency and you have bliss; take the nostalgia of reason away and the world is neither meaningful nor absurd—it merely happens.

3. THE INDELIBILITY OF EVIL

If the world is contingent, evil is merely one of the facts of life with which the mature person must learn to live. Any attempt to give an explanation of evil is bound to fail. Thus, modern philosophy has given up the traditional quest for a theodicy which occupied a central place in past philosophical and theological thinking.

Idealism was never wholly successful in explaining evil. Someone has said that the problem of evil is the "rock on which all philosophies and all theologies shipwreck." Explanations, no matter how logically air-tight, have always faded into insignificance before the senseless brutalities of war, the ravages of flood and disease, and death's relentless thievery of love. Yet, though every explanation has failed, an important part in the creation of the Western attitude toward life has been played by the ever recurring effort to build philosophical and theological structures within which a life of hope could be shown to be reasonable. Thus, the traditional idealistic affirmation that evil is penultimately but not ultimately real—that the forces making for order and meaning in the cosmos are finally more powerful than the forces of chaos—represents the refusal of the human spirit to capitulate before death and tragedy.

The solutions to the problem of evil offered by various forms of idealism in the Western tradition differ in detail but are fundamentally variations on a common theme: evil, if seen (1) from the vantage point of the Absolute Mind *above* history, or (2) from the perspective of God at the *end* of history, is overcome or neutralized as it blends into universal harmony or into the cosmic plan of God. Various analogies have served as models for explaining evil. The aesthetic analogy has been the most common: what appears from a historical perspective to be evil is, from the mountaintop observatory of the Absolute, like the dark shadow that provides the necessary contrast in an otherwise beautiful picture. Appearances to the contrary, this is, as Leibnitz said, "the best of all possible worlds." Another dominant analogy is the "obstacle-course" view of the maturation of the human soul. The world, so this argument goes, is a "vale of soul-making." Without the possibility of doing evil there could be no possibility of doing good, no freedom, and no personality. Since a world peopled by free agents is superior to one without freedom, the evil that is instrumental to the development of moral freedom is justified. Those persons who have suffered injustice, tragedy, and unhappiness through no fault of their own will be recompensed in a future life. Hegel made an interesting variation on the obstacle-course theory in maintaining that negativity was necessary to the development of the Absolute Mind. Hence, evil existed only from the limited perspective of one caught in one phase of the Absolute's self-development. Evil is the necessary price we pay for helping the Absolute come to self-awareness.

Why is it, we must ask, that these analogies and theodicies, which once served to buttress the affirmation of the human spirit that evil does not cast the last stone in the universe, now ring so hollow? Why do we find it hard to believe that anything could possibly erase the indelible record of evil from human history? The current feeling about the finality of evil does not arise from any quantitative increase of it. Man's inhumanity to man and nature's carelessness are the warp and woof of history, past and present. The root of the matter seems to lie in the conviction that existence in a contingent world provides no timber for constructing an observatory from which the whole of history can be seen in perspective. Relativism and skepticism regarding man's cognitive powers spell the end of theodicy. If neither myth, nor reason, nor revelation gives us knowledge of an eternal order, we are left with only the tragic flux of history. The contemporary vision of man is formed by and limited to history. Man has no wings on which to soar to the mountaintop of the Absolute or to the transhistorical throne of God. Time is real, and we are her children. We *are* our limited perspective, and we will not sell the heritage of earth for the promise of eternal pottage. To admit that "in the long run" or "in God's overall plan" or "from the Absolute's perspective" Auschwitz may figure positively in the overall good of man is to falsify our experience of the meaning of good and evil in human history. If some eventual nostrum can erase the indelible stains of evil, if some future plus can balance the past minus, then human history as experienced and lived is transvalued. We have no way of thinking about the meaning of such a transvaluation. If the lion does lie down with the lamb, we are no longer talking about those animals we now call lion and lamb. When we start to examine the possible meaning of the neutralization of evil—the eventual cosmic harmony and other "solutions" to the problem of evil—we find that thought and imagination evaporate into thin air and we are left holding only words devoid of their normal meanings.

No more vivid illustration of the shift in the attitude toward evil can be given than a comparison of two accounts of hangings of innocent men, one given by Melville in the last century and the other an account from a survivor of Auschwitz. Billy Budd, the innocent, almost Christlike young sailor, was condemned to death by Captain Vere for striking Claggart, the Master-at-Arms. Claggart's death was virtually an accident, and both Billy and Captain Vere admitted the injustice of the sentence given Billy. Yet the last words of Billy Budd as he goes to hang are "God bless Captain Vere!" Evil is present, but it does not triumph; benediction, forgiveness, and testimony to good arise out of and transcend the tragedy. Compare with this affirmation of good in the midst of evil the account of Elie Wiesel in his book, *Night,* which records his experiences as an adolescent prisoner in Auschwitz.

I witnessed other hangings. I never saw a single one of the victims weep. For a long time those dried-up bodies had forgotten the bitter taste of tears.

Except one. . . .

One day when we came back from work, we saw three gallows rearing up in the assembly place, three black crows. Roll call. SS all around us, machine guns trained; the traditional ceremony. Three victims in chains—and one of them, the little servant, the sad-eyed angel.

The SS seemed more preoccupied, more disturbed than usual. To hang a young boy in front of thousands of spectators was no light matter.

The three victims mounted together onto the chairs.

The three necks were placed at the same moment within the nooses.

"Long live liberty!" cried the two adults.

But the child was silent.

"Where is God? Where is He?" someone behind me asked.

At a sign from the head of the camp, the three chairs tipped over. Total silence throughout the camp. On the horizon, the sun was setting.

"Bare your heads!" yelled the head of the camp. His voice was raucous.

We were weeping.

"Cover your heads!"

Then the march past began. The two adults were no longer alive. Their tongues hung swollen, blue-tinged. But the third rope was still moving; being so light, the child was still alive.

For more than half an hour he stayed there, struggling between life and death, dying in slow agony under our eyes. And we had to look him full in the face. He was still alive when I passed in front of him. His tongue was still red, his eyes were not yet glazed.

Behind me I heard the same man asking: "Where is God now?"

"Where is He? Here He is—He is hanging here on this gallows."

That night the soup tasted of corpses.[8]

Wiesel goes on to record his loss of belief in God and his self-imposed exile from the religious community, which went on proclaiming the praises of the God they believed to be concerned with them even in their unjust sufferings.

This day I had ceased to plead. I was no longer capable of lamentation. On the contrary, I felt very strong. I was the accuser, God the accused. My eyes were open and I was alone—terribly alone in a world without God and without man. Without love or mercy. I had ceased to be anything but ashes, yet I felt myself to be stronger than the Almighty, to whom my life had been tied for so long. I stood amid the praying congregation, observing it like a stranger.[9]

Evil here is completely unredeemed, for the faith has been lost that man has any vantage point from which he may affirm anything other than the complete meaninglessness of such tragedy. The conviction grows, and Camus has articulated it for a whole generation, that to be a man is to stand in the face of indelible evil, abandoning all illusions and hopes for a transhistorical solution, and fight with abandon against the plague of injustice and suffering. All attempts to rationalize or explain evil, all theodicies, must be abandoned, as they lull man into the illusion that evil is somehow confined, limited, and conquered in principle if not in fact. Contingency consists of the recognition that evil is real and the idealistic visions of harmony are but a whistling in the dark which frequently become a substitute for trying to relieve the darkness.

4. THE "DEATH OF GOD"

THE GOD OF NATURE AND THE GOD OF HISTORY

Certainly the most dramatic symbol of Western man's changed self-understanding is the notion of the "death of God." When cosmic reason was replaced by technical reason, the God of the cosmos died; the vision of the holiness resident in the order of the universe ceased to inspire men. While modern scientific man is aware of the intricate order of the subatomic and astronomical worlds, he finds no moral significance in it. Order is merely a fact; it is not evidence of a moral intention resident within things. The physical world of modern science is orderly but not teleological;

it is law-abiding but not a sphere of revelation. Thus, the divinity of the cosmos is no longer.

As I suggested in the last chapter, many Christian theologians (such as Karl Barth and Harvey Cox) have insisted that the loss of the God of the cosmos and the death of the divinities of nature are to be applauded rather than lamented. The true God is revealed in history rather than in nature. The Judeo-Christian God can live even when all intuition of the divinity of nature is lost. In fact, the dedivinization of nature represents the death of an idol which allows the revelation of the true God in Jesus Christ to become more obvious.

This line of argument, which has characterized Protestant theology for the last thirty years, refuses to face the radical nature of the changes in Western self-understanding and hence the seriousness of the issue of the death of God. Faith in the God of revelation of the Judeo-Christian tradition is no less threatened or rendered questionable by the changes in the modern consciousness than is the God of the cosmos. The God who revealed Himself in history is as vulnerable as the God who revealed Himself in nature. There are at least three factors that contribute to the growing inability to give credence to the traditional Christian concept of God.

First. The whole notion of revelation has become questionable because of the radical historical and literary critcism of the texts of the Old and New Testaments and the increased knowledge of Hellenistic religions. In spite of theological rejoinders to the contrary, the uniqueness and validity of Biblical religion have been called into question. Knowledge of the history of dogma destroys the illusion that what the contemporary Church holds to be orthodox theology can be traced back to the New Testament community, much less to the self-understanding of Jesus. The "revelation" of Christianity turns out to be an amalgam of Jewish apocalyptic and Gnostic redeemer myths which coalesces around a prophet-teacher whose history is largely unknown. Modern man, finding the images, symbols, and world view of first-century Palestine alien to his experience, takes some of the ethics of Jesus as good counsel but can make little sense out of the central claim of traditional Christianity that God definitively revealed Himself in Jesus

Christ. The Christological path to God which the contemporary "death of God" theologians in common with Karl Barth and Harvey Cox have all tried to defend is, if anything, even more dubious for modern man than belief in a God who reveals Himself in the cosmos.

Second. Belief in the Judeo-Christian God is threatened also by the rise of urban culture and religious pluralism. Twentieth-century society is religiously pluralistic, and the revelational claims of many religions, pseudo religions, and antireligions must compete on the open market. It is not the case, as Barthian theologians have charged, that there are many religions but only one revelation. Every live, momentous option in a pluralistic society presents itself as a revelation of what is most ultimately true. Christianity must take its place beside psychoanalysis, Marxism, Zen Buddhism, secular humanism, 100 per cent Americanism, and many others as a system of belief that claims to present a true path toward integration and authenticity. The sensitive person in our society asks himself how these different claims to truth are to be adjudicated. Which "revelation," which path to salvation, is to be followed? From questioning springs doubt and skepticism about the possibility of arriving at any adequate view of the ultimate truth about things. That such questioning and doubt exist is sufficient evidence that the God of the Judeo-Christian tradition, no less than the God of the cosmos, is threatened with death. Or, to be less dramatically metaphorical, the holy power that gives assurance of the intrinsic dignity and meaning of human life is no longer encountered by the majority of Western people in the God of the Judeo-Christian tradition.

Third. Perhaps the most serious threat to the Christian tradition comes from a widespread alienation of religious affections. Most persons in Western culture who are nonreligious waste no time in active rebuttals against God. It is merely that the religious climate has changed and the romance of modern man is with the earth and not the gods or God. There was no particular moment when it became intellectually impossible to believe that the cosmos was a holy teleological system or that Jesus was the definitive revelation of God. Indeed, many people continue to hold such beliefs. Our age, however, is fascinated with mastering and controlling the immediate environment and has little interest in questions about the ultimate significance of human life; penultimate concerns are dominant and ultimate concerns are unconscious or repressed. As a friend of mine who gave up doing theology to return to industry said, "I have given up trying to unscrew the inscrutable." The dominance of pragmatic, operational modes of thinking spells trouble for religious beliefs and institutions, because it reflects a switch in spiritual loyalties. What more damning critique of the Judeo-Christian concept of God could be offered than the yawn it receives at a time when enthusiasm (note the etymology!) runs high for discovering better ways to make cities humane and more effective modes of therapy to heal the hurts of the psyche?

We must conclude that the "death of God," the loss of the sense of the presence of the holy, affects equally the vision of the divine cosmos that we inherited from primal and Greek man and the Judeo-Christian understanding of the invasion of history by God in certain mighty acts. Both cosmological and historical wonder are eclipsed by modern self-understanding.

THE MEANING OF THE "DEATH OF GOD"

Perhaps the best place to begin is with the epistemological problem—with the changing estimate of the limits of human knowledge. Traditional man was convinced that there were *techniques of transcendence* which gave access to an eternal order of reality. These techniques were diverse, ranging from primitive magic and rites of divination to sophisticated, dialectical philosophy of the Greeks to prayer, meditation, and Bible-reading in the Judeo-Christian tradition. A common assumption upon which all these techniques rested was that man was an amphibious creature belonging to two orders, the temporal and the eternal, and he could have adequate knowledge of both. It is the collapse of this conviction that is responsible, in part, for the atrophy of the experience of God. Religious "knowledge" is widely considered mere emotionally tinged morality or the projection of psychological need. It would not be too much to say that the concept of the death of God results from the loss of the idealistic view of reason and the collapse of the credibility of prayer. When man ceases to believe that he has some means of communication with God, then the concept "God" has only ceremonial and metaphorical usage and is without existential significance. Peter Moen, a Norwegian patriot imprisoned by the Gestapo, recounts an experience of an unsuccessful search for faith which is typical of many modern men.

"With a sad sigh I must state that the experiment gave a negative result. I found no anchor-ground for faith or conviction of anything divine speaking to me or in me. I found the *wish* for its existence but this wish is quite explicable from the point of self-preservation and egotism. I can only find that my altogether honest attempt led me back to my standpoint of twenty years: No truth is found outside man. *Everything* originates with man himself and that includes all thoughts and feelings concerning God."[10]

Even within the Christian community prayer has become difficult. Bishop Robinson reports what is certainly the experience of many: prayer as communication with God is meaningless and must be replaced by an understanding of prayer as opening oneself to the world and the other person who is encountered. While encounter and openness are certainly to be desired, popular piety is correct in charging that Robinson's view of prayer is a capitulation rather than a reinterpretation. Prayer as a technique of transcendence is inseparable from belief in God. Where the ability to use human language in the presence of what is experienced as ultimate is lost, it is because the conviction has vanished that there is any *analogy* between the human mind and that source from which all things flow. Since the idea of analogy is the heart of religious faith, when it disappears, so does the belief in God.

[*purification of religion* — handwritten margin note]

While most contemporary atheism results from lack of interest in the question of God, a militant antitheism is also obvious, especially in the intellectual community. If we may speak of God dying from neglect, we must also speak of His being killed. Eliade has spoken of the consistent secular man as one who experiences the sacred only as a barrier to freedom. Secular man "makes himself, and he only makes himself completely in proportion as he desacralizes himself and the world. The sacred is the prime obstacle to his freedom. He will become himself only when he is totally demysticized. He will not be truly free until he has killed the last God."[11] When God becomes a "senile adolescent delinquent"

(Tennessee Williams) or the "ground of repression" (Nietzsche, Altizer) or an excuse for not joining battle with evil (Camus), he must be destroyed before authentic human freedom becomes possible.

It is in the philosophy of Sartre that the most consistent and aggressive antitheism is to be found. He is, by Eliade's definition, the completely secular man, for he sees in the idea of the holy only an obstacle to human freedom. It is not merely that he denies that God exists, although he does hold that this is a necessary starting point for existentialism. The more radical rejection of the sacred comes in Sartre's denial that there are any essential structures inherent in man. Man is completely free to create his own values; there is nothing in heaven or on earth to which he must bow. "We have neither behind us, nor before us in a luminous realm of values, any means of justification nor excuse. We are left alone, without excuse."[12] The complete neutrality of the world is necessary as an environment for human freedom. If there are any "oughts," any given standards of good or evil, or any invasions of human life by powers beyond its control, there is no freedom. Thus, in the name of freedom, the holy is banished from the world. "God is dead" is equivalent to "man is totally alone and free."

Certainly most people in Western culture have not become secular to the extent that Sartre has. Few have his courage to push down the semidivinities—which at best support a life of gentle boredom and despair—and proclaim a new, virile humanism. If most have lost confidence in the God of the cosmos, they have retained their allegiance to little gods. This piecemeal polytheism allows for gods on rainy days without the embarrassing demand for total commitment. While it is impossible to make any accurate list of live and dead minor gods or of extant and extinct areas of holiness in contemporary experience, some generalizations may be risked. For most men in the Western world, the "great god Pan is dead," as D. H. Lawrence declared; the woods no longer speak to us of Artemis, nor do "the heavens declare the glory of God." Nature does not radiate a Presence; it provides us with the raw materials to be converted into artifacts which we desire. The most universally adored god would seem to be Aphrodite. Love is the sole savior, the only guarantor of security, happiness, and meaning in an alien world. If two can become one, they may stand together against the emptiness. Such seems to be the conclusion of the majority of modern movies, plays, and novels. The holy is still experienced by some in the quest for artistic creativity or in the fight for social justice. Whatever the area in which the experience of the holy survives, it remains for many an island of meaning in a sea of meaninglessnes, a moment which remains unintegrated into any total system of meaning. In traditional culture, the idea of God functioned to integrate all experienced values in some hierarchical fashion; it provided a way of assuring man that he lived in *a* universe or *the* kingdom of God. The death of God means the establishment of pluralism as an ultimate fact of existence. Moments of holiness there may be; romantic love, work, or the nation may become "ultimate concerns," but no single allegiance integrates these moments into a consistent philosophy of life.

5. CONCLUSION: THE ECOLOGY OF MODERN MAN

What kind of a world is it in which contingency has replaced reason, in which evil cannot be understood or rationalized, and in which all authority for establishing norms and values resides in the creative power of the human will? How does man experience the envelope of space and time, of nature and history, within which his decisions must be made?

As the idealistic vision disintegrates and is replaced by the totally contingent world, the ecology of the human spirit changes. The world is no longer experienced as giving support to human purposes and values or as mediating a transcendent purpose. But if the world is not friendly, neither is it alien. Nature is neutral— "blind to good and evil." Hans Jonas has compared contemporary nihilism with the negative evaluation of the world that arose shortly before the Christian era and was most clearly expressed in Gnosticism.

There is no overlooking one cardinal difference between the Gnostic and the existentialist dualism: Gnostic man is thrown into an antagonistic, anti-divine nature and therefore anti-human nature, modern man into an indifferent one. And only the later case represents the absolute vacuum, the really bottomless pit.

This makes modern nihilism infinitely more radical and more desperate than Gnostic nihilism ever could be, for all its panic terror of the world and its defiant contempt of its laws. That nature does not care, one way or the other, is the true abyss. That only man cares, in his finitude facing nothing but death along with his contingency and the objective meaninglessness of his projected meanings, is a truly unprecedented situation.[13]

The ecology of modern man is the vacuum; he is weightless, with nothing to push against; he must form his identity in a void. The universe is neither caring nor alien—only neutral. Nothingness is the final word about the nonhuman world. "Our nada who art in nada, nada be thy name, thy kingdom nada, thy will be nada, in nada as it is in nada. . . . Hail nothing, full of nothing, nothing is with thee." The ultimate category governing human existence is not grace but *chance*. Life is not a gift but a happening, and any individual exists not because of any benevolent intention but because of the chance coming together of mindless particles. In the empire of chance, prayer and thanksgiving are replaced by knocking on wood, throwing salt over the left shoulder, or some such liturgy offered to Lady Luck.

With the ecology of human existence changed for some and changing for others, what kind of new models will man find to understand his life? Being no longer *homo sapiens, homo admirans,* or a creature in the image of God, who is modern man? What kind of plant will grow in the desert soil of the empire of chance? To the question of the new model of self-understanding arising from the realization of contingency we now turn.

This future man, whom the scientists tell us they will produce in no more than a hundred years, seems to be possessed by a rebellion against human existence as it has been given, a free gift from nowhere (secularly speaking), which he wishes to exchange, as it were, for something he has made himself.

—HANNAH ARENDT[1]

CHAPTER V

The Travail of
Homo Faber

As the rains from heaven have dried up and the once fertile soil of earth has blanched before the merciless sun of absurdity, the human plant has changed its form to adapt to the arid conditions of what Camus called the desert of nihilism. When the spiritual chemistry of the soil supporting human life changed, man's image of himself underwent transformation. While ours is an age of confusion, anxiety, and pluralism, there is a developing consensus concerning the nature of man; there is *an* image which, although not unanimously accepted, is central to modern self-understanding.

The major theme of this chapter will be that the image of *homo faber* is the key to contemporary identity. Our task will be to construct a typology which will make clear the essential structure of this image and exhibit in outline its presuppositions, strengths, and weaknesses. The reader must bear in mind that a typology is an artificial construction designed to show the logical integrity of some phenomenon. There are, of course, many competing views of man in the modern world, and all of them cannot be harmonized. Nor does any individual flesh-and-blood person think, feel, or act on the basis of one consistent set of presuppositions. Thus, no typology will clarify and organize all phenomena any more than a net of one size will catch all the fish in the sea. My claim is merely that when *homo faber* is taken as the central organizational image of modern man, we are able to understand more than with an alternative image, and in particular, we are able to discover the rationale behind the eclipse of wonder and make proposals for its recovery.

A minor theme also runs throughout this chapter. When man is understood exclusively as *homo faber,* a spiritual schizophrenia results in which there is an oscillation between omnipotent and impotent feelings and expectations. This schizophrenia is evidence of the pathological functioning of the image of *homo faber* and points to the necessity for a broader image of man, which I shall sketch in a final chapter. Since our analysis will center around certain cryptotheological claims of *homo faber,* let us look at (1) the process which led to his assumption of omnipotence, and (2) its relation to feelings of impotence.

1. THE ATTEMPTED APOTHEOSIS OF *HOMO FABER*

THE ASSUMPTION OF OMNIPOTENCE

It is with varying degrees of optimism and anxiety that modern man has taken upon himself the responsibility for creating values and ends which traditional man assumed were homogenized into the cosmos. Some, like Nietzsche, have greeted the new task with rejoicing and a heightened sense of human dignity. In a world devoid of transcendent norms and authorities man is suddenly free for himself; he has come of age. Gone is the childish subservience to myth, revelation, and symbols or institutions that claim unconditional allegiance (with the possible exception of The State). At first it was only the atheistic thinker—such as Feuerbach, Marx, or Freud—who assumed the Promethean stance and greeted the dawn of complete human responsibility with joy. Later, however, even Christian theologians joined in. Bonhoeffer began the trend with his cryptic letters from prison in which he suggested that man had "come of age" and must learn to live in the world as if there were no God. Altizer, Hamilton, and Van Buren, the so-called "death of God" theologians, added their voices to the chorus, demanding that man free himself from dependence on illusions of transcendence and take full responsibility for creating and implementing his own values on the open sea of adventure. Interestingly enough, it has been the unequivocal atheist who sounded the note of sorrow and spoke of the terrible burden and anxiety of complete human freedom. Sartre, Camus, and Heidegger all testify to the anguish of total responsibility, while the death-of-God theologians are far more optimistic about the potency of human freedom.

But whether the mood in which total responsibility has been accepted has been one of enthusiasm or anguish, the dynamics governing the resultant understanding of man are identical. Once man takes upon himself the task of creating a meaning for life and history, he assumes both the burden and the privilege traditionally assigned to God. As Feuerbach stated, in true humanism (which is the philosophy of *homo faber*) the predicates of God are transferred to man, theology is replaced by anthropology, and man becomes both the subject and the object of theology. Since the defining characteristic of *homo faber* is his assumption of the task of creating meaning, any analysis of his aspirations must center around his cryptotheological claims.

Homo faber became a central image of modern man as a direct result of the collapse of belief in the creative and informing power of a transcendent God. If God, cosmic reason, or any surrogate for these traditional divinities does not give life meaning, then man himself must take over the task. This basic assumption of *homo faber* is captured in Eric Fromm's remark: "If man faces the truth without panic he will recognize that there is no meaning in life except the meaning man gives his life by unfolding of his powers, by living productively."[2]

Once again the earth is without form and void and darkness is upon the face of the deep, but now the spirit of man must move across the face of the waters to create a world and invent a meaning for life. Like the Demiurge in Plato's philosophy, man finds an inchoate world of raw material which must be given meaning and value by being fabricated into artifacts useful for maintaining life.

For the most part, *homo faber* does not consciously or publicly demand that the predicates of God be transferred to man. A measure of reticence and innate modesty prevents all but the most brashly insensitive from self-conscious deification of man. It is no longer considered good form, as it was in the eighteenth century, to publicly depose God and place man on the throne of the cosmos.

For this reason the dramatic antitheism of Sartre and the death-of-God theologians seems quaint—an antique gesture. However, a functional atheism may be discovered in the basic images and models of man that command the majority allegiance in our time. The omnipotent claims of modern man are hidden in advertising slogans, in methodological statements, in misplaced hopes and dreams, and in unexamined maxims which form the basis of action. The twentieth century is atheistic in practice but not yet in rhetoric.

The Realization of Impotence

Something of the failure of the effort to apotheosize *homo faber* is obvious when we acknowledge the existence of a cluster of impotent images of man which is significantly operative in contemporary culture. Edmund Fuller, commenting on the view of man in modern fiction, laments the whole spate of modern novels in which man is seen as "an ironic biological accident, inadequate, aimless, meaningless, isolated, inherently evil, thwarted, self-corrupting, morally answerable to no one, clasped in the vise of determinisms economic or biological."[3] This cluster is composed of images that show man as a victim rather than a victor, subhuman rather than superhuman, a captive rather than a captor. Man's impotence has been dramatized under a variety of metaphors and language games: Dostoevski and Kafka showed man turned into an insect or an animal; Marx showed him reduced to an economic commodity; various positivists, determinists, and behaviorists reduce him to a nexus where cause and effect, stimulus and response, meet; D. H. Lawrence and Koestler use sexual impotence as symbolic of modern man; Camus paints an unforgettable portrait of alienation in *The Stranger*.

These impotent images spring from the same change in spiritual ecology that gave rise to the omnipotent images; however, they represent a different response to the crisis. The Promethean humanism of Nietzsche and the architects of new technological utopias represents an optimistic response to the challenge to build a truly human city in the desert of meaning which has resulted from the death of God. The tragic humanism of Kafka, Beckett, and Ionesco has been far less sanguine about the human possibilities. Deprived of the gift of power and meaning which once came from the transcendant world, the tragic humanist has been overwhelmed by a sense of abandonment, anguish, and anxiety and has questioned man's potency to create a world sufficiently rich in meaning to make life tolerable. The responsibility for creating may be man's, but he lacks the power.

2. THE ANATOMY OF *HOMO FABER*

MAN: HOMO FABER OR HOMO FABRICATUS—
ARCHITECT OR ARTIFACT?

Homo Faber

There are four separable but interrelated meanings which contribute to the definition of man as *homo faber*.

First. Man is the animal who makes and uses tools. The history of human dignity began on the day when an adventurous ape discovered by some happy chance that the thumb could be used to grasp a stone, which in turn could be used as a weapon or a tool. Once the tool was created, incipient man was no longer a slave to the fickle graces of nature. His primitive tools, and later his sophisticated technology, gave him the power to reshape his environment. The tool changed man from a passive recipient to an agent, from a child to an adult, and changed the world of nature from a gift to raw material. This literal meaning—man as defined by his technology—is the most usual significance of the term *homo faber*.

Second. The human mind, no less than the hand, is a toolmaking and tool-using faculty. As pragmatism, operationalism, and behavorism have stressed, man's ideas and symbols are tools which allow him to handle and cope with the world. The brain is to the world of spirit what the thumb is to the world of matter—an instrument for molding and controlling. Since symbols are tools, there can be no incompatibility between the ideas of man as toolmaker and as symbol user. All artistic, religious, and philosophical symbols are means of fabricating world views which are necessary instruments to guard against the excessive intrusion of chaos. Man must make a structure of ideas within which to dwell, no less than he must construct a city to insure rational and orderly satisfaction of his needs. This is dramatically illustrated in a recent *Denver Post* account of a speech by Emmanuel Mesthene, the director of Harvard's program on technology and society:

Religion satisfied the very human need to celebrate and glory in the fact that man can know, and see and unify. And since celebration and glorification are social activities, men are acting religiously when they join together to worship a common vision of what man could be if he were so fully human as to be physical man no longer. It is easy to see how such a vision can generate the myth of a personal God. . . . If God emerges as the essence of making and of purposing, it may be possible to make the step back from the myth to the vision and to see God as a celebration of what man might be as ultimate maker and purposive being—for example, as pure artist. To so see God is to see that man has made Him with his tools. Nor is it blasphemy, I think, to interpret God as the greatest creation of man the tool-maker.

It is easy to see in this pragmatic view of religious symbols the reversal of the judgment of traditional man. Man now creates the idea of God as a covert way to glorify his own ability to make tools and make meanings. Symbols are no longer words somehow saturated with the ultimate power that informs all things, the *logos,* but are instruments which may be turned to any purpose man desires. Symbols do not reflect reality—they create it; thus the word is still creative of all meaning, but now it is the human word. Words have replaced *logos* as the creative agent.

Third. The chief product of *homo faber* is man himself. Man makes his destiny by creating an identity for himself and by manipulating the world to coincide as nearly as possible with his desires. While traditional man could always find some concrete and authoritative model of the authentic life (e.g., Socrates or Jesus), *homo faber* has no a priori authority to guide him, hence he must invent himself. Existence must precede essence, as Sartre has said. Modern identity springs, thus, from the will, the project, or the decision rather than from a vision of an ideal. By projecting goals into the future, *homo faber* becomes the teleological mind that orders and gives meaning and value to things. Any event or thing may be assigned a value in relation to its significance for the projected goal which *homo faber* has decided to make the meaning of his life. The final dream of *homo faber* is to design and consruct man without the obstruction of a fatefully imposed past or psychic structure, to mold existence to coincide with an essence which is chosen rather than given.

Fourth. In its most degraded and popular form, the image of *homo faber* signifies that man is a worker. If at best *homo faber* is purely creative, at worst he is compulsively active. Under the impact of the techniques of mass production, creativity has been increasingly identified with work, and work with productive activity. Thus, to discover the influence of the image of *homo faber* we must look at the significance work has for personal identity in contemporary society.

In spite of the encroaching menace of leisure, the secularized Protestant ethic of work continues to provide a central focus of identity for the majority of Americans. If the spirit of capitalism had a voice, it would speak as Ayn Rand does.

Your work is the process of achieving your values, and to lose your ambition for values is to lose your ambition to live. . . . Your body is a machine, but your mind is its driver, and you must drive as far as your mind will take you, with achievement as the goal of your road. . . . Your work is the purpose of your life, and you must speed past any killer who assumes the right to stop you. . . . Any value you might find outside your work, any other loyalty or love, can only be travelers you choose to share your journey and must be travelers going on their own power in the same direction.[4]

For *homo faber* there is no vocation except work because there is no God who can appeal to man. Man must manufacture his own dignity by working. Under the impact of industrialization, creativity gives way to work, occupation, and production. It is for this reason that we find the most concentrated points of identity-crisis in our society where we find persons ostracized from the world of work—the preemployed, the unemployed, and the postemployed. Those who are excluded from the arena in which values and meanings are produced are exiled from full humanity. Work gives status and identity (except among those groups which are systematically excluded from more meaningful jobs because of prejudice).

It will do no good to condemn the Protestant ethic of work or to offer a shallow critique of American activism (let the

French teach you the value of wine and leisure, and from Zen learn the lesson of doing nothing). Activism and the work ethic are rooted in basic presuppositions about the nature of man; they do not result from stimulated adrenal glands or wider opportunities. The same change has taken place in thinking about human substance that took place in thinking about material substance. With the discovery of radioactivity and the dynamic structure of the atom, substance became process, mass became energy, and matter became motion. Scientists no longer think of any essence or underlying substance that is unchanging. A thing is what it does; its identity is its history; its being is process. These same assumptions increasingly govern our understanding of man. We commonly ask a person to whom we are seeking to relate: What do you do? (What is your job—what function in society do you fulfill?) Thus the activism of *homo faber* is rooted in the striving to become human. Since being human means becoming human, the dignity, value, and meaning of human existence are to be won only in action. Subtract the action and you have no being; apart from the process there is no substance. Hence, *homo faber* is active not to occupy time but to find salvation. We are justified by our actions, by our fabrication, by our work. Any legitimate critique of the activism of American culture will have to root in some model of man which makes appropriate (i.e., grounds ontologically) modes and moments of human existence which are unrelated to making, doing, fabricating, or acting.

Homo Fabricatus

Who is the master and who is the servant? Has man, in fact, as *homo faber* contends, dominion over his machines, or has he become the victim of his own creation? Of course, there is no clear answer to this question. Here the way divides between the technophiles and the technophobes; the machine has its priests and its enemies in both aristocratic and vernacular cultures. We are concerned here with describing rather than reconciling the opposing views. Whatever the reality of the situation, the feeling is common that man is increasingly a victim of his technology.

In vernacular culture the resentment against the domination of the machine has been expressed in figures such as Charlie Chaplin in *Modern Times*. In an unforgettable way he dramatized the inhuman results of forcing man to conform to the rhythm of the machine. On the assembly line man becomes only another part of the machine, and a poor one at that—always breaking down and hampering the efficiency of the process by allowing grief, joy, or fatigue to invade working hours. The continuing nostalgia for the pastoral life that pervades American literature and the Western movie, would seem to point in the same direction—the machine-dominated man is less than authentic.

At a more sophisticated level, thinkers such as Lewis Mumford and Jacques Ellul have suggested that modern technology may have begun to operate in terms of an autonomous imperative that is not responsive to human values. The machine is out of control and man is in the position of responding to what is technically possible but humanistically undesirable. A new sense of fatedness, parallel to that which gripped Greek societies, seems to be arising. We are becoming victims of the impersonal logic of the machine. Consider, for instance, the function machines have had in creating a new human type—the consumer. Increasingly, American culture is geared to mass production and mass consumption of artifacts and commodities which serve no biological need. Our economic system is dependent upon planned obsolescence, the stimulation of artificial desires by advertising, and forced consumption. The new man is an insatiable consumer, force-fed by the machine on commodities which must be successfully marketed for the good of the economy; his arteries are clogged with cars and cholesterol, resulting in those characteristically modern forms of stoppage: the traffic jam and the heart attack. One wonders whether the most appropriate image of the function the machine fulfills in our culture might not be that of the Jewish mother ("Have a fourth helping of" an electric toothbrush, battery-powered knife, automatic shoeshine kit, cocktail stirrer). It is as if our culture were plugged into the mechanical tit of a machine which force-feeds it until it begins to produce waste. *Homo faber* has become a "waste maker," the anus of the machine rather than its brain. A more lethal example of the machine's inhumanity to man may be seen in the escalating spiral of weapons technology. When missiles become possible, antimissiles must be manufactured, and then anti-antimissiles, and anti-anti-anti-antimissiles, etc., ad infinitum! Technical possibility becomes political necessity until that apocalyptic moment when humanity as a whole becomes the victim of its machines and the population of the Western world consists of one radioactive rabbit and two computers talking to each other over red telephones.

To move, however, from the dramatic to the mundane, there is a growing fear that machine culture may have more subtle means of dehumanizing man. Man may be becoming increasingly like his products; he may be making himself over in the image of the machine. Gabriel Marcel has noted that the categories of "function" and "output" are increasingly applied to man. "The individual tends to appear both to himself and to others as an agglomeration of functions. As the result of deep historical causes . . . he has been led to see himself more and more as a mere assemblage of functions."[5] He goes on to suggest that a functionalized world is one from which mystery, wonder, and the sense of the intrinsic significance of being are lost. When the categories of function, efficiency, and output become central for identity, the result is alienation; the individual no longer feels himself to be a sacred nexus of life. Karl Marx, over a century ago, predicted that capitalism would increasingly turn man into an alienated worker whose life was governed by the necessities of technology. Seemingly the repressive factor in technology may lie more in the manner in which we internalize and identify with the model of the machine than in the economic and class power which Marx thought machines would give to the bourgeois. When the machine became a fixture of everyday life in the industrial revolution, philosophy began to abound with machine analogies. "Man the machine" was not only the title of a popular book but a master model. Currently, as the computer revolution is in full swing, the computer analogies are invading philosophy and psychology. The human mind is "data processing," knowledge and emotions may be "programed," "feedback mechanisms" are essential for the psychocybernetic system of man to operate, and so on.

How are we to tell the story of *homo faber*? Who is the maker and who the made? Perhaps this is the way the story should be told: man begins to create a new image of himself and a blueprint for the world, and he ends up creating himself in the image of the world that happens as a result. If he perceives the world to be pervaded by, or invaded by, the gods or God, he will try to create himself in the image of God; if his world is perceived as inchoate raw material waiting to be given form and value by technological intelligence, then man will become a technocrat and will reflect the image of the machine. The ambivalent judgments relative to *homo faber* indicate, at the very least, the fear that man's ability to free himself from the bondage of nature by use of the machine may lead to another form of slavery.

THE OMNISCIENCE AND FOLLY OF HOMO FABER

Omniscience

Having assumed the predicate of omnipotence, *homo faber* must either claim or aspire to omniscience, for, as medieval theologians knew, power and knowledge are inseparable. This observation was put into a maxim by Francis Bacon which may serve as a summary of the faith of technological man: "Knowledge is power."

Man's aspiration to omniscience is as old as the race. Long before Western civilization was defined by machine technology, the Faustian urge expressed itself in the mystical quest for union with God and in the philosophical search for a coherent and adequate knowledge of the whole of reality. *Homo faber* inherited the struggle for omniscience most directly from the Enlightenment. There are three assumptions of the Enlightenment view of man which continue to inform *homo faber*. (1) Man is fundamentally a rational being and, hence, may be governed by an ever increasing knowledge of the world. (2) Education and investigation are the twin paths to knowledge and salvation. And (3) the present generation is the hinge of history; it has come into the light of reason and left behind the darkness of superstition, myth, and ignorance; in the education of the human race it has passed from the stage of childhood to maturity. It should be clear that *homo faber* has accepted and expanded these basic assumptions. Belief in the ultimate intelligibility of the universe and the potency of investigation and analysis is the cornerstone of science. Education and investigation are the most prestigious activities of modern culture. That man has in our time "come of age" is so common an assumption that theologians can join with teen-agers in the suspicion that no one over thirty can really escape the archaic ignorance of the past and understand what is happening in the post-McLuhan age of electronic circuitry.

The contemporary quest for omniscience, although sharing the Enlightenment view of man, has its own unique features. The instrument we look to for enlightenment is no longer the ahistorical, universal reason of which Kant spoke, but rather the pragmatic, operational, analytical faculty of technical reason. The two most characteristic forms of the modern aspiration to omniscience are found in scientism and positivism. In both cases completely adequate knowledge (and therefore power) is thought to result from the application of "the method of science" to philosophical and practical problems.

The aspiration toward omniscience which is reflected in scientism and positivism rests upon the reduction of human thought to a tool which may be manipulated to yield solutions to problems. Progress in knowledge is inevitable, since one solution builds upon another as complex tools depend upon the mastery of more simple tools. The critique of *homo faber*'s aspirations toward omniscience grows out of the questioning of the adequacy of the technological model of thought.

. . . and Folly

Opposed to the optimistic estimates of man's evolution toward omniscience, there is a growing body of opinion and judgment which pronounces *homo faber* a learned fool. To call a man a fool is not necessarily an insult, for the authentic life has frequently been pictured under the metaphor of the fool. In figures such as Socrates, Christ, and the Idiot of Dostoevski we see that foolishness and wisdom are not always what they seem to be. To the worldly-wise, the philosopher and the saint always appear foolish and incompetent, if not positively demented. The bourgeois laughed at Thales for being so lost in wonder and contemplation that he fell into a well, and they laughed at the political naïvete of a "messiah" whose power involved voluntary acceptance of suffering. Underneath the incognito of the clown, wisdom has frequently been detected. The accusation against *homo faber* is not, however, that he is a wise man who appears a fool but that he is a fool who pretends to adequate knowledge.

The voices are many which charge that we live in a time of the eclipse of wisdom and may well die of philosophical and spiritual malnutrition, in a society which is the greatest data generator ever known. "Where is the wisdom we have lost in knowledge?" Eliot asks us. And the Vermont farmer to whom Steinbeck talked on his trip through America put his finger on the same problem.

My grandfather knew the number of whiskers in the Almighty's beard. I don't even know what happened yesterday, let alone tomorrow. He knew what it was that makes a rock or a table. I don't even understand the formula that says nobody knows. We've got nothing to go on—got no way to think about things.[6]

The problem is not merely that we have lost confidence in old answers, but the traditional methods of arriving at wisdom, the techniques of contemplation and transcendence, have become incredible, and no new ones have arisen to take their place. Neither in philosophy, in theology, nor in literature do we have satisfactory methods for answering the most persistent *why* questions. The wisdom that once anchored man in the flux of time has become an historical relic, and we are adrift in the stream of change without purpose—in the whirl of Heraclitus from which the structures and paths to wisdom have disappeared. No way to think about questions of ultimate concern which refuse to be banished—this seems to be the dilemma of *homo faber.*

Homo faber is charged with responsibility for the eclipse of wisdom because of his exclusive confidence in a type of thinking that systematically denies cognitive status to poetry, religion, and metaphysics. As Chesterton noted, there is a form of madness which consists in using thought to stop thought, in using mental activity to stop mental activity, and—we may add—in using knowledge to deny wisdom. Although wisdom involves reflection on empirical data, it can only flourish where the climate of reverence for mystery allows contact with the indistinct but vivifying symbols and myths that traditional man used to articulate his vision of the world. Wisdom necessitates a confession of belonging to a universal community of man and, hence, a denial of the Enlightenment assumption of the radical discontinuity between present knowledge and past ignorance.

The insistence that clarity is the only modality of authentic thought likewise destroys wisdom. Clarity is necessary to both thought and action, but the demand for absolute clarity may root in a compulsive need for security which destroys the organic indistinctness and mystery of things in order to gain intellectual certainty. Clarity is to the life of the mind what germs are to the life of the body—too much or too little destroys life, just as an antiseptic environment fails to build up the immunity necessary to health. Thus the obsession with clarity is the scrubbing compulsion of the mind—a defense mechanism to guard against the threat of the chaotic mystery of life. While *homo faber* has dispelled many of the demonic ghosts of ignorance, he has at the same time fallen prey to the pretension of omniscience, to the foolish pride of believing that he can eliminate the mystery of being. And there is something both sad and comic in the sight of the modern intellectual who keeps trying to banish the ultimate *why* questions—and the dramatic, mythological language with which they have traditionally been answered, from the honored categories of thought and knowledge—because he cannot get any purchase on them with his prehensile tool-using mind. *Homo faber* has become all thumbs.

Wisdom has traditionally been the possession of the old because only age brings the patience to let things happen in the ripeness of their own time. Reflection on past experience leads to confidence in the organic interrelatedness of things. *Homo faber* is committed to making things happen, and one of his major projects is maintaining the state of changeless youth. Since aging, illness, and death are evidence of the failure to control, they must be disguised and ignored. Thus the worship of youth, which precludes the development of wisdom, leads to the prolongation of adolescence into "mature" years and desperate efforts to hide the cancerous effects of time behind a façade of dyed hair, lotions, potions, and changing styles.

HOMO FABER: LORD OR ENEMY OF NATURE?

The success of *homo faber* has led to a change in the way man thinks and feels about his relation to nature. Pretechnological man was able to domesticate so small a portion of the earth that he lived in constant fear of floods, drought, disease, or the silent perils of the wilderness. As modern technology has domesticated broader reaches of nature, man has graduated from the status of child of nature and increasingly experiences himself as the executive, master, or lord over nature.

It is important to bear in mind that we are dealing here with images of self-understanding. The center of our concern is not the question: Is *homo faber* lord over nature? We are concerned less with the fact of control than with the *rhetoric* of control. How do we think and feel about the control we are able to exercise over nature and about the "natural" world we control?

With the escalating advances in technology, we have undergone another revolution in our thinking about man's relation to nature. We have reached the point where we imagine that man has ceased to be a product of evolution and has become its producer. Human intelligence and technology may determine the direction of the future evolution of man. In a recent article on "The Crisis in Man's Destiny" Julian Huxley defines the status of modern man.

A new vision has been revealed by post-Darwinian science and learning. It gives us a new and assured view of ourselves. Man . . . has become the latest dominant type in the solar system, with three billion years of evolution behind him and (if he doesn't destroy himself) a comparable long period of evolution before him. . . . His role, whether he wants it or not, is to be the leader of the evolutionary process on earth, and his job is to guide and direct it in the general direction of improvement. . . . We need no longer be afflicted with a sense of our own insignificance and helplessness, or of the world's nonsignificance and meaninglessness. A purpose has been revealed to us—to steer the evolution of our planet toward improvement. . . . The final aim will be the eugenic transformation of his social environment.[7]

Lest this clearly omnipotent hope for lordship over nature be thought to reflect only secular humanism, we may remind ourselves that it does not differ significantly from the vision of the Catholic theologian Teilhard de Chardin. De Chardin finds in modern economic, industrial, and social changes the evidence that a change in the noosphere has taken place which will henceforth make the evolutionary process come under the direction of human intelligence. Man is, in his words, "the arrow pointing the way to the final unification of the world."

Many persons who retain either a romantic or a religious view of nature would be loath to adopt the rhetoric that affirms man's lordship over nature; yet in practice they act upon the same assumption. Actions constitute a pragmatic confession. Let us contrast two different ways of acting in regard to nature and see the implicit confessions being made in each. Symbolic of one relationship to nature is a proposal made recently by Edward Teller before the American Physical Society. According to Teller we should explode a nuclear bomb on the moon in order to find out what its interior is made of. This proposal is of a piece with the explosion of an atomic "device" (never "bomb") in the Van Allen Belt; the indiscriminate use of penicillin, DDT, cigarettes, and tranquilizers; and the dumping of waste material into streams and airways. All these actions are based upon the unarticulated maxim: *There is no wisdom resident within the ecology of nature* (interior or exterior)—there is no natural law, no order of nature that man is obliged not to violate. Man's relationship to nature is one of dominion; his manifest destiny is to subdue nature and make it conformable to his desires. As symbolic of the second attitude, we may consider the movement toward conservation of forest and mineral resources advocated by groups like the Sierra Club. When we undertake systematic reforestation and preservation of wilderness areas, we confess in action that man and nature offer each other mutual succor only when man restrains his impulse to superimpose human patterns on the whole world. This second attitude involves the almost archaic notions of respect and communion and denies that utilization is the only appropriate category for thinking about nature.

The metaphors "lordship over nature" and "executive responsibility for nature" suggest a relationship of oversight, management, and control. A lord exercises dominion over his estate as an executive wields power and imposes rational management upon his organization. In the Western religious tradition "lord" also bears the connotation of one whose power to govern is both rational and loving. The logic of these metaphors thus raises the question of their appropriatenes to characterize man's relation to nature. Two questions might be asked: Does man exercise dominion over nature? Is the dominant attitude toward nature one of either rational oversight or sympathetic concern?

Although it is difficult to know exactly what degree of control over nature would be sufficient to make the use of "lord" or "executive" appropriate titles for *homo faber,* it should be clear that there is a vast gap between the rhetoric of control and the fact of control. At the same time that we talk blithely of a future world in which nature will be completely domesticated, we continue to live prey to the excesses of weather and to the rhythms of growth and decay. The ultimate victory still belongs to nature rather than to technology, for the machine can, at best, only postpone the victory of dust over flesh.

One may wonder whether *homo faber's* disappointed demand for omnipotent control is not responsible for his viewing nature as an enemy. Although romantic feelings toward nature survive in a sufficiently large portion of the population to make Walt Disney's nature films among the most popular forms of entertainment "for the whole family," there seems also to be a revival of a gnostic feeling about nature. *Homo faber* shows contempt for what he has been able to master and hostility for that aspect of nature which he has been unable to control. While we can infer no strict causal relationship between disappointed expectations of omnipotent control and abuses of nature, when we see a redwood forest reduced to a stubble, a stream filled with industrial waste, etc., it is *as if homo faber* were taking revenge against an enemy who had revealed his weakness. The hostility between man and nature is graphically illustrated in a recent article by Eric Hoffer entitled "A Strategy for the War with Nature."

Man became what he is, not with the aid of, but in spite of nature. . . . Humanization meant breaking away from nature, getting out from underneath the iron necessities found in the newspapers, in the almost daily reports of floods, fires, tornados, blizzards, hurricanes, typhoons,

hailstorms, sandstorms, earthquakes, avalanches, eruptions, inunda-
tions, pests, plagues and famines. Sometimes when reading about
nature's terrible visitations and her massacre of the innocents it
seemed to me that we were surrounded by devouring, pitiless forces,
that the earth was full of anger, the sky dark with wrath, and that
man had built the city as a refuge from a hostile, nonhuman cosmos.
I realized that the contest between man and nature has been the central drama of the universe.[8]

Why is it that we receive such gnostic sentiments, which are
clearly only half the truth about nature, with such readiness and
are so suspicious of romantic attitudes? Why should Hoffer recount
only the terrors of nature—the earthquakes and typhoons? What
of the "blue flowers and the merlin's flight and the rime on the
wintry trees, blue doves . . . and summer light on the wings of the
cinnamon bee"?[9] Primitive man also knew the terrors of nature,
but he was able to celebrate "her" graciousness. Again, the semi-
fantastic category of the *as if* may provide the best clue. In spite
of having achieved a degree of control over nature that was un-
dreamed of by traditional man, *homo faber* can celebrate nothing
less than the omnipotent power to structure life in absolute conformity with his desires. Since nature continues to frustrate man's
manifest destiny—his claim to absolute control—"it" can only be
seen as an enemy that must be subdued.

Homo faber does retain a type of truncated wonder in the face
of nature: before its facticity and power he experiences awe and
terror, but not admiration. We might call to mind the famous
scene in *Nausea* where Antoine Roquentin confronts the tree. The
nausea he experiences reflects his inability to reduce the being of
the tree to a set of meanings that fit into the world he has constructed for himself. The tree is "superfluous" (de trop), for it
eludes the effort of Roquentin's mind to reduce its significance to
a meaning comfortable to his project. The existence of things that
cannot be fitted neatly into the world of human projects is an
insult. Thus, nature is like a sticky marmalade that clings to man
and nauseates him. In this experience of the strangeness of nature
there remains an element of wonder as *tremendum* but not as
fascinans. We must ask ourselves whether *homo faber*'s inability

to experience the givenness of nature as admirable does not root in his systematic refusal to recognize value in anything he has not fabricated.

HOMO FABER: ARCHITECT OF THE NEW JERUSALEM?

It is not strange that *homo faber* should look upon nature either as raw material to be utilized or as an uncontrolled surd to be feared, since his normal habitat is the city. The birth and growth of the city parallels the development of the machine, and *homo faber*'s dreams for the future are for a city as harmoniously and efficiently functioning as a giant machine. As a house has become a "machine to live in," the city of the future will become the megamachine, and as cities grow they will become coordinated into an overall design for "ecumenopolis," the world-wide city.

There is a principle which makes the secular city the appropriate expression of the hopes of *homo faber:* all must be brought under control. The city is man's way of controlling his external environment, of living in a space which he structures to coincide with his own needs and desires. Recently it has become clear that the principle of control can be applied to the internal environment as well as exterior circumstances, and thus *homo faber* has begun to dream of a future in which both inner and outer space will be subject to complete rationalization and choice. Between city planning and psychochemistry, man will be able to live in a completely chosen environment.

In order to gain a more concrete picture of the hopes of *homo faber,* let us look at some predictions about the future of technological man that are being made by serious scientists. Some possibilities now within the range of conceivable technological development are as follows.

1. Cities will cover most available land and will be planned to make possible harmonious development of mind, body, and soul.

2. The economic system will be controlled to produce all consumer needs with a minimum of labor; hence, the productive use of leisure will be the chief vocation of future man. Education, the arts, and the development of meaningful personal relationships will be the major concern of the masses.

3. Increasing use of communication media and rapid transportation will bind all civilized countries together into one world community, which will force an end to nationalism and war.

4. Interplanetary travel and inhabited artificial satellites will be common.

5. Populations will be stabilized, and food production will coincide with need.

6. Disease and famine will be eliminated.

7. Complete control of human emotions (the interior environment) will be possible by chemical means, thus eliminating mental illness and anxiety.

8. Knowledge may be stored in "electronic banks" and transmitted directly to the human brain without passing through consciousness, thus eliminating the need for concentration and mental labor.

In even so brief a list it is easy to detect the shape of the New Jerusalem, the eschatological city of the saved, in the blueprint of the secular city of the future which *homo faber* has drawn. All toil, pain, poverty, and fear will be eliminated from Technopolis. Man will create a city in which there will be no estrangement, a utopia free from all the negativities that have haunted the existence of traditional man. In this vision man has become the savior of man and the tool has replaced the cross as the instrument by which the promised kingdom will be ushered in. Should *homo faber* desire an appropriate ritual to symbolize his faith, he might well replace the Catholic custom of making the sign of the cross with the sign "Thumbs up!"

One awkward contour of the human condition continues to frustrate *homo faber*'s aspirations to be an architect of the New Jerusalem—death. In the projected city of the future all the traditional enemies of man have been conquered save one. And as the New Testament reminds us, "the last enemy to be destroyed is death" (I Cor. 15:26). Unfortunately, the inability to solve the problem of death throws a question over all the promises of the new technological Jerusalem. A city filled with every delight which has been unable to ostracize death is still a city ruled by tragedy, needing both wisdom and grace to sustain its life. The more deeply we love life and enjoy full vitality, the more we feel, with

Augustine, that "anything that ends is too short." It is not accidental that the repression of the awareness of death is to the twentieth century what the repression of sex was to the nineteenth. A culture animated by technological hopes is unable to face the problems of death because it throws into question the values and goals for which it strives. Few prophets of the New Jerusalem have been bold enough to predict victory over death—to declare that the machine will make us immortal; but negotiations are now in process. It is commonplace to suggest that life may be prolonged by abolishing known diseases and replacing damaged or malfunctioning organs of the body. Recently it has been suggested that those suffering from presently incurable diseases might be quick-frozen and later thawed, when a cure has been found. While the possibility of such immortality-on-the-installment-plan does not seem imminent, that it can be suggested reveals the eschatological aspirations of *homo faber*. Even mortality and death must not be considered a permanent limit. The full-blown dream of *homo faber* is charted by no less a scientist than Augustus Kinzel, president of the Salk Institute.

If we look to the long-term future we see a still greater impact of technology on both civilization and society. As for the external environment, we will have electricity from heat, wireless transmission of energy, and new materials, such as nonorganic polymers and the like. As for the internal environment, we will be really able to manipulate the DNA molecule and to predetermine heredity. We will lick the problem of aging completely, so that accidents will be essentially the only cause of death. We will be able to design supermen.[10]

Only the details of this charter and the agents responsible for its implementation have changed from the traditional Christian vision of the New Jerusalem.

When the covert omnipotent claims and aspirations of *homo faber* are brought to light it is easy to understand what has happened to wonder in the modern world. Wonder is still experienced in relation to the holy, only now the manifestations of holiness are the power and products of technological intelligence, are not the divine *logos* which the ancients saw operative in nature and history. *Homo faber* still makes his religious pilgrimages to the sacred precincts in which his hopes are incarnate—in which his vision of the future is celebrated. The World's Fair and Expo 67 are both examples of meccas which *homo faber* periodically consecrates and visits in order to wonder before the most advanced technology and renew his vison of the Jerusalem he will create in the *very* near future.

Homo faber is encountering both practical and theoretical difficulties in constructing the New Jerusalem. If the city presents a new freedom which allows association to develop by choice rather than chance, it also breeds anonymity, rootlessness, and loneliness. The same New York that draws aspiring artists from the cloying atmosphere of small Iowa towns into the intoxicating diversity of Greenwich Village watches, fearful of involvement, while Catherine Genovese is murdered. The Harlems and Wattses testify clearly that *homo faber* has so far failed to create even a human city, much less a superhuman one. Ugliness, travail, tragedy, alienation, disease, and death continue to exercise the largest vote in the council of the secular city.

It is frequently argued that while, in fact, there are many remaining pockets of frustration, violence, and degradation, these may in principle be eliminated from the city of the future. The fault lies not with the utopian blueprint but with the failure to use present knowledge and power to rehabilitate the city of man. While there can be no question that, were the energies wasted in warfare by *homo furens* applied to *homo faber*'s project of creating the perfect city of man, we would be able to eliminate many sources of alienation and tragedy, it remains to be seen whether or not there are fundamental inadequacies in the blueprint itself. Every utopian scheme (and seemingly every projection of the cybernated future is either utopia or apocalyptic—either integrated harmony or universal destruction) hinges upon the application of universal, centralized control. A completely rationalized and controlled environment necessarily involves a control center. In political terms the blueprint for the New Jerusalem rests upon the assumption of a totalitarian dictatorship more stringent than anything the world has yet known. If a total society is to function as one harmonious unit, someone has to regulate population, see that supply and demand coincide, and program the physical and emotional climate to insure maximum happiness. All "realistic" political utopias have their commissars, Grand Inquisitors, central planning councils, and so forth. Brave New Worlds and great societies must have their architects. It is when we consider the architects and the principles upon which they propose to construct the New Jerusalem that the fundamental inadequacy of the model of *homo faber* appears.

The twentieth century has shown us sufficient genocide, mass murder, uprooting of entire populations, and slave labor so that we ought to be aware that precisely those leaders who see themselves as "makers of history," as "architects of a new order," are most likely to create hell on earth. It is the "programatic revolutionary," as Camus called him, who is animated by a vision of a dictatorship of the proletariat, or a pure fatherland, or a world committed to the American way of life, who is willing to sacrifice the lives and happiness of any number of present generations for the realization of a future ideal. To the architect of history the people of the present are mere raw material to be used in constructing the dream city. Any number of gassed Jews, murdered bourgeois, or napalmed villagers are justified to create the alabaster city of the future which will be undimmed by human tears. Human beings, like the neutral materials of the natural world, are means to whatever end the maker of history has defined.

It is not accidental that when *homo faber* becomes the architect of the political order he is the committer of atrocities against the tender fabric of the human community, for he has no basis for a theory of community except the will to power. Value and meaning arise from projects of the will. Thus, a political mass must be molded by the imposition of an ideal, and it is to be expected that there will always be resistance to overcome. *Homo faber* has no theoretical basis for a community based upon respect for the integrity of present man. The principle of respect rests upon some intuition of the sacredness of the given. Traditional religions have said that community was a gift of the gods and that civility between citizens was therefore an ultimate religious duty. Even as the traditional religious justification for community began to wane, the sacredness and integrity of citizenship was preserved by demythologized religious concepts like "the inalienable right to iife, liberty, and the pursuit of happiness," and by various social contract theories. Whether overtly religious or based upon social utilitarianism, past justifications for community have rooted in the wondering intuition of the sacredness or inviolability of man as *a present and given phenomenon*. The worth of being human was not, for traditional man, contingent upon being incorporated into some five-year plan or great society. The impotence of *homo faber* to create a truly human community, even while he dreams of utopias, follows from his refusal to admire, and therefore confess, the sacredness of anything that is merely given. All data are raw data, meaningless until fabricated into a product which has been willed and chosen.

3. FROM *HOMO FABER* TO *HOMO LUDENS?*

The technological success of *homo faber* has created a new historical possibility—a reversal of the hierarchy of work and leisure. Where leisure was once the privilege of an elite which had to be supported by the slavery or toil of the masses, it appears that in the foreseeable future leisure will be the common condition of the mass, and labor may be the privilege of the few. Traditional man was able to dream of a leisure society and was even able to define man as *homo ludens*. Plato could say, for instance, that because men were the playthings of the gods, "life must be lived as play, playing certain games, making sacrifices, singing and dancing." However, until the advent of modern technology, the bulk of mankind was forced to labor with little relief. The machine now promises to lift the burden of toil from the shoulders of man and leave him free to realize his ancient dream of becoming *homo ludens*.

In dealing with an image such as *homo ludens,* we must separate the fact from the interpretation. The successes of *homo faber* have, in fact, within a century made it possible for most persons in Western society to procure the biological necessities of life with the use of a minor fraction of their available time. Measured by hours free from the necessity of work, Western man now may claim the title *homo ludens* as more appropriate than that of *homo faber*. It still remains to be seen how *homo faber* interprets and understands the significance of his work and play. *Homo faber* may in fact and in self-understanding become *homo ludens,* or he may be unable to give up the "theology" of work even when it becomes economically unnecesary. We shall examine these two possibilities in turn. Our concern is not to trace the growth of leisure but to see how we understand the significance of work and leisure.

An immediate impression gleaned from the quantity of literature in which leisure and play are considered central human vocations would seem to suggest that the image of *homo ludens* is beginning to assume great importance for Western identity. Both Huizenga, the Dutch historian, and J. Pieper have suggested that play is central to culture; the metaphor of "games" has assumed central significance in philosophy (Wittgenstein) and in psychology (Berne), as well as in education and strategic planning for war and diplomacy; businessmen are justifying their commitment by insisting that work is really a game; the playboy has replaced Horatio Alger as the model for under-thirty Americans. Evidently learning, earning, and yearning may all be functions of play. Increasingly, we are warned that we must prepare for shorter work weeks, early retirement, and shortage in available work by developing a leisure ethic for an affluent society. Play is to replace work as the definitive human vocation.

In order to flesh out the logic of the image of *homo ludens,* let us examine its most popular manifestation—the playboy.

It is clear at once that the ideal types portrayed in the pages of the magazine *Playboy* are not primarily defined by work or job. While the man who reads *Playboy* makes well over the median income, his attachment to work is peripheral. Freed from physical need, the life of the playboy becomes effortless play, erotic spontaneity, and dangerless adventure. There are two foci of play: consuming and romantic-sexual activity.

Both the advertisements and the "Playboy Advisor" make it clear that the game of consuming has rules that must be rigidly followed. The playboy must be an expert on the latest styles in clothing, automobiles, wines, and all luxury appliances; he must know whether to stir or to shake a martini. The category that governs his consumption is what is "cool" or "in" (synonyms: chic, hep, hot, camp, tough—characteristic of the category is that the language changes yearly). Moral concerns do not create any anxiety for the playboy, but the possibility of being discovered "in bad taste" creates the specter of shame—how embarrassing to quote the wrong authors, serve the wrong wine, be caught with old-fashioned "repressive" views on sex, or the like. While the rules of the game are shifting and nebulous, they are every bit as demanding as more formally ordered games. As Allen Wheelis has pointed out in *The Quest for Identity,* the requirement that one must adjust to the shifting tastes and opinions of a peer group involves sensitivity to what is happening and endless flexibility. Eternal vigilance is the price of acceptance.

The chief vocation of the playboy is erotic play. Sex is the essence of fun, to be enjoyed in any form which is mutually pleasing to any two consenting participants. In this play-oriented view of sex, mystery, tragedy, and failure are notable by their absence. In his relationship with women, who are all 36-24-35 and without blemish, underarm odor, or asymmetrical development, the playboy is gay and omnipotent. There is never a hint that upon occasion between the potency and the act "falls the shadow," that sadness may still desire, that hatred and tenderness may be strangely mixed, or that love may sometimes flame when flesh grows cool in age or cold in death. The playboy is perpetually twenty-seven, young but not foolish, expert in fun and fornication but hardly in love, and hip but not involved. In the image of the playboy the Olympian gods have returned to earth; the enjoyment of wine, women, and song in an albaster city untouched by human distress has become the vocation of man.

While the rhetoric of *Playboy* suggests that sex has become the supreme form of fun for *homo ludens,* there is a growing body of opinion which suggests that exactly the opposite may be true—the playboy philosophy of sex as play may conceal the effort of *homo faber* to use his genitals as "tools" to forge out an identity. Is it possible for sex to be play for *homo faber* or does it inevitably become work? The landslide of "how-to-do-it" books aimed at instructing the novice player in the techniques of sex would suggest that, while sex may be developing into a highly organized game, it has lost much of the spontaneous character of fun (a distinction I shall comment on shortly). Psychiatrists such as A. Lowen and Rollo May report a high degree of anxiety concerned

with performance and adequate mastery of the techniques necessary to be a good sexual partner. When sexual performance becomes a focus used to establish identity, it ceases to be fun and
becomes compulsive work. It may be that for *homo faber* "sex
has become the 'one green thing' in a world of steel and calculation, and therefore more desperate, more fearful of impotence,"[11]
but there is also a logic implicit in the model of man-the-maker
which renders play-ful sex (as well as all play) emotionally inappropriate. Sex involves mutual giving; as play, it is a dance of
generosity and acceptance. *Homo faber* is a maker and a trader;
therefore the acceptance of a gift has no place in his world. As
Ayn Rand has commented, the authentic individual is a trader;
he is neither a looter nor an altruist; he gives fair exchange. In
sex, as elsewhere, the ethical questions become: Did I make a
good trade? Did the accounts balance out? Did I give as much
satisfaction as I received? Clearly such an attitude makes playful
sex, in which generosity rather than calculation is central, impossible.

Apart from the difficulties the present generation is having in
achieving a genuinely playful attitude toward sex, there is the
broader problem of what can only be called the threat of leisure
and play. *Homo faber* seems to be tyrannized psychologically by
work even when it is not an economic necessity. There are many
indications that work remains a central focus of modern identity
even when the content of the work and the personal associations
involved in it are not satisfying. Robert Dubin's study of the "industrial workers' world" suggests that three out of four industrial
workers "did not see their jobs and work places as central life
interests for themselves. They found their preferred human associations and preferred areas of behavior outside of employment."[12]
Yet another study of industrial workers reported that 80 per cent
would go on working even if there were no economic need, although the job itself was without meaning or positive satisfaction.[13]
These studies point to the problem of alienated leisure. Even when
work has ceased to be economically necessary, creatively satisfying, or the focus of meaningful personal relationships, it remains
a psychological (or should one say "theological") necessity. Both
the remnants of the Protestant ethic of work and the ideology of

homo faber conspire to create the hidden maxim which makes genuine leisure impossible—"Meaning, dignity, and value are the products of work, and legitimate leisure is always a reward of work." For *homo faber,* leisure is reduced to (1) *recreation,* which is the work-free time necessary to prepare a man to go back to work, or (2) *reward* for work accomplished. Genuine leisure is literally "free time" and depends upon the notion that time (and therefore human existence) is in some sense a gift, but *homo faber* is unable to accept what is free. Hence, time off from the job in excess of what is necessary for recreation becomes a burden and an embarrassment. The superfluous gift of time is something *homo faber* knows he has not earned, so he "kills it" or fills it with trivia. Leisure becomes alienated for *homo faber* because he harbors guilt for accepting something he did not earn. In order to accept time as a gift, and therefore enjoy leisure, he would have to give up the maxim that is the key to his identity.

Another indication of *homo faber*'s inability to come to terms with play may be seen in the contemporary theory and practice of games. The game is the only way *homo faber* is able to play; it is a sublimation of the fun instinct. It is noteworthy that in the classic study of *homo ludens,* Huizenga begins by stating that the element of "fun" is central to play, but as his study continues the agonal (contest) element becomes dominant. *Homo faber* conceives of play in terms of structure and discipline. There are two characteristics of games that make them comfortable ways for him to deal with the need for fun: (1) games are organized, structured, rule-governed, workful play, and (2) games, as they have come to be played in contemporary culture, are contests, hence continuous with the competitive spirit of capitalism.

Conspicuously absent from game-oriented play is the element of spontaneous fun which is not rule-regarding. When we think of the way small children play we get a valuable clue to the relation between fun and games. Piaget has observed that for three-year-olds, rules and standards are almost nonexistent in play; five-year-olds see and sometimes respect rules; for seven-year-olds, rules are sacred and immutable. Thus, young children's play is governed by the logic of delight and is spontaneous, but older children tend more toward inventing games that mimic the adult world and so are rule-governed. Wherever *homo faber* finds himself outside of boundaries and rules he has erected, he gets anxious; thus pure play is threatening because it is spontaneous and an end in itself. It is interesting, in this connection, to note the number of articles and books on play in children that emphasize the utilitarian function of play. Play is okay because it teaches children skills and roles and is a necessary prelude to socialization; it is justified because it is useful. Such a constipated view of play obviously rests upon a deep gnostic suspicion which considers delight, pleasure, and fun acceptable only if they are means to some other end. In refusing to honor the spontaneous delight of the senses which is the essence of unstructured fun, *homo faber* reveals a hatred of matter and flesh and, hence, of the erotic. He reserves his eros for the structures and products which he can create and control—for the works of his own physical and mental thumbs.

The dominance of games at the cost of fun and enjoyment was illustrated to me in a recent incident. In walking to work I pass a large field which has several horse-chestnut trees around its edges. As fall approached, I watched daily for the first pods to fall and disgorge the gleaming, chocolate-rich nuts, anxious that the hordes of boys who played on the field should not rob me of the pleasure of fondling a few "worthless" chestnuts and enjoying their incomparable brownness. To my amazement, I discovered that my anxiety was needless. One day, after a week's absence, I found the ground littered with chestnuts, undisturbed; a hundred feet away several Little League teams were practicing with the dedication of professionals—blocking, tackling, and punting—too busy to hoard chestnuts or even engage in an impromptu battle. After stuffing my pockets I walked away, and I imagined I heard the coach of one of the teams shout to a couple of boys who strayed too near the trees, "Leave those damn chestnuts alone, and let's get on with this game!" In the kingdom of Apollo games are permissible, but fun and undisciplined enjoyment, belonging properly to Dionysus, are suspect.

For traditional man, leisure was bound up with the holy and the wonderful. On holy days he remembered and celebrated his kinship in an eternal order with the gods, and on ordinary days he paused to contemplate the mystery of meaning and order that pervaded the cosmos. For *homo faber,* leisure has ceased to mean the opportunity to celebrate or contemplate and has become time to be filled with games centering on copulation, consumption, and competition.

4. REFLECTIONS ON THE SCHIZOPHRENIA OF HOMO FABER

When the image of *homo faber* is taken as *the* organizing focus for understanding man, it fails. I have suggested that it is inadequate to integrate the growing possibilities of leisure, to provide an appropriate philosophical foundation for understanding spontaneous play, to allow for an appreciative and nonutilitarian encounter with the world of nature, and to understand the element of giving in sex (as opposed to "making out"). The image of man as *homo faber* is so exclusively "masculine" that it makes impossible an appreciation of the dignity of the more "feminine" modes of perceiving and relating to the world; it majors in molding and manipulation and neglects accepting and welcoming. Thus, it renders wonder and all those attitudes which cluster around it inappropriate.

Before we can suggest how the image of *homo faber* may be incorporated into a view of man that will allow us to make more sense of both the "masculine" and the "feminine," we must seek to understand more clearly the logic involved in its failure. The pathology of *homo faber* must be explored to allow us to get to the heart of the error that is responsible for the schizophrenic feelings and expectations this image has generated in contemporary culture. The application of the notion of pathology to cultural rather than merely individual problems is not new. Fromm and Horney have pointed out that images, no less than economic institutions or political policies, may function in a neurotic fashion. My thesis is that the image of *homo faber* functions in contemporary society in a neurotic fashion, and the task is to understand the dynamics of the neurosis.

According to Karen Horney, neurosis results when the imagination and energy of personality are directed toward the creation of an "idealized image" rather than toward realization of the actual possibilities of the self. Self-idealization leads to a "search for "glory" and a demand for unlimited power, knowledge, love, perfection, etc. Although these unlimited demands can never be achieved in reality, they form the script which the neurotic follows. Self-hatred results from the failure to achieve the fantastic degree of perfection and power which the idealized self sees as its birthright. The neurotic is in a double bind: he is filled with self-hatred because of his inability to live up to the hero script he has constructed for himself, yet he is unable to give up his fantastic ideals and become interested in the nurturing and growth of his real self, because this would mean giving up his claim to superiority, invulnerability, and glory. It is far better in his eyes to be a miserable god than a satisfied human. Thus, the dynamics of neurosis center around the oscillation between hidden claims to glory and self-loathing—between feelings of omnipotence and impotence. The missing element in the neurotic personality is recognition and appreciation of an appropriate sense of *limits*. In periods when the feelings of omnipotence are dominant the neurotic becomes, in imagination, unlimited—a Faust; in periods of self-hatred he is unable to take any comfort in the concrete but limited possibilities and achievements of the real self. As Horney says, "Every neurotic at bottom is loath to recognize limitations to what he expects of himself and believes it possible to attain. His need to actualize his idealized image is so imperative that he must shove aside the checks as irrelevant or nonexistent."[14]

Although this rendition of the theory of neurosis is far from complete, it is sufficient to allow us to see the neurotic manner in which the image of *homo faber* functions in our culture. I have shown the omnipotent expectations and claims of *homo faber,* ranging from the pretense that man alone is creative of those structures that introduce value and meaning into the cosmos to the promise that technology will usher in a New Jerusalem, in which future man will be free from tragedy and limitation. The destiny of MAN is to be glorified, without disease, war, or anxiety—living in perfect harmony in an ideal environment. This, *homo faber* tells us, is who we are, and if the dream is still just a few generations beyond our reach, that is no reason why we should not appropriate it to our self-understanding. But—let us turn our eyes from the future of MAN to the present of men. Despite the promise of new hearts and kidneys for old, of anxiety-free existence, and of near-immortality, we continue to sweat and grow old, to be haunted by fears, and to succumb to diseases of the mind and body. Alongside the glorified MAN which the technological future has promised us, we remain so pathetic and insignificant. We remain individual men and women, bogged down in Watts and Vietnam, still pathetically dying of diseases which will one day be curable and suffering from anxiety attacks and identity problems which will one day be chemically eliminated.

The distance between the glorified man that *homo faber* promises and the flesh-and-blood man of the present is so great that we are led to despise the actual. Like neurotics dreaming of who we might become, we come to despite who we are. How can we not hate the fragile flesh that brings both pleasure and death, when we are—in promise if not in fact—heirs to the life of the gods in the New Jerusalem just around the corner? Is it any wonder that, alongside the promise of the future superman, we find images which show man as insect, animal, and victim? When we fail to be all, we become nothing; when we become disillusioned with our efforts to live in the heavens, we become "underground" men.

In the last century Feuerbach, Marx, Nietzsche, and later Freud charged with vigor that the Christian idea of an overworld and the whole of idealistic philosophy, which they saw as a weakly demythologized religious vision, were destructive of human dignity. Promising "pie in the sky," or its philosophical equivalent of an absolute perspective from which the tragedy of history vanished in the life of the Divine Spirit, theologians and philosophers seduced men into abandoning the possible satisfactions of the real world. The hope of eternal perfection and the claim to transcend the ambiguities of history turned man aside from taking responsibility for shaping human society in more satisfactory ways and from enjoying the fleeting, sweet fruits of the sensual earth. The existentialist critique of Christian eschatology and idealistic philosophy rightly saw that idealized images of man frequently root in resentment and hostility toward his actual condition. In contemporary culture the eschatological promise of *homo faber* has replaced Christianity and idealism as the source of the idealized image of man. So far as they tempt us to despise our actual condition and make it impossible to consider concrete existence a gift, the promises of *homo faber* function to degrade rather than enhance the quotidian. No matter how comfortable technology makes life, it still destroys human dignity if it holds before us an image which inevitably shows up present man as inauthentic in light of the future perfection of MAN. A curious historical irony may be in the making: science and technology, which emerged only when men began to love the earth more than the heavens, may be leading us to despise the actual because of the possible. If this is the case, we need a Kierkegaard who will remind our time that the tenuous balance of human dignity is destroyed if we forget to love either necessity or possibility—the tragic limits of the present or the open possibilities of the future.

At the root of the neurotic self-understanding of *homo faber* lies the failure to come to terms with the connected notions of *limit* and *gift,* hence, with that mode of perceiving and celebrating which we have been calling wonder. To be is to be something; to accept oneself and the world is to accept limits which are prior to and unalterable by individual decision. The world into which any existing person emerges is already richly informed with meaning and value. Before I begin to choose, I am already shaped by being male, white, middle-class American, and having a certain range of available energy and intelligence, tastes, opinions, aspirations, and so on. To accept myself is to accept the limits as gifts— not as unalterable, but as the specific shape my existence bears at the moment when it first becomes conscious of the responsibility for deciding and defining new limits for itself. The resentment against all a priori limits (the necessity of death or the givenness of value) by *homo faber* reflects a hostility toward the givenness of human existence which is merely the reverse side of the refusal to admire, to wonder, and to be grateful. Limits, *for homo faber,* are merely the rules of the game, which may be changed at will— products of his intellectual and physical tools which may be altered by more advanced tools. Such a view is deeply alien to the wisdom implied in Pascal's statement: "Man is something but he is not everything." The authentic life involves recognition and celebration of limits and possibilities. To a closer definition of authentic life we may now turn.

This at least seems to me the main problem for philosophers. . . . How can we contrive to be at once astonished at the world and yet at home in it? How can this world give us at once the fascination of a strange town and the comfort and honour of being our own town? . . . We need this life of practical romance; the combination of something that is strange with something that is secure. We need to view the world as to combine an idea of wonder and an idea of welcome. We need to be happy in this wonderland without once being merely comfortable.

—G. K. CHESTERTON[1]

CHAPTER VI

Wonder and
Authentic Life

The central question with which this chapter deals is that of the place of the attitude of wonder within the healthy or authentic personality. I will suggest that healthy personality involves a balance between receptivity and manipulation, between wonder and action. Wonder, therefore, can only be adequately understood when it is seen within the economy of the total personality.

The notions of health, maturity, and authentic life, which are here used interchangeably, are normative rather than descriptive. Observation alone will not yield a model of authentic life. While any intellectually responsible person tries to give his allegiance to an ideal of man which evidence and experience show to be reasonable, there is an element of risk, commitment, and recommendation involved in any philosophical account of authentic life. Definitions of man, hopefully, have a factual basis, but they are also statements of faith as well as dispositions to act in a given way.

Our proposal will be that the authentic man is best understood as *homo tempestivus,* the timely, seasonable, or opportune man. Thus far our analysis has dealt with two primary models that typify traditional and modern man, *homo admirans* and *homo faber.* We shall see that *homo tempestivus* provides a synthesis of virtues of these models without falling prey to the spiritual dependancy of *homo admirans* or the Promethean pride of *homo faber*.

Our method for constructing a model of authentic life will involve an analysis of the Apollonian and the Dionysian modes of being in the world. While there are many conceptual schemes one might use to organize models of man which are live, momentous, and forced for the present generation, I have chosen this typology (which was used with great power by Nietzsche) because it reflects the radical alternatives that *seem* to confront the young: either repressive order or undirected violence, either conformity or rebellion, either surrender to the system or turning on, tuning in, and dropping out; either work or ecstasy, either discipline or freedom, either abiding commitments or spontaneity, either the ego or the id, either the past and the future or the present, and so forth. We are, in fact, experiencing a rebirth of the Dionysian option and a radical questioning of the model of man as *homo faber* (a basically Apollonian model). It is important in this moment of transition to evaluate the strengths and weaknesses of both Apollo and Dionysus. While I have been suggesting throughout this book the necessity of wonder for authentic life, it may be possible to have too much wonder. Wonder is basically a Dionysian attitude; thus, our use of this typology will allow us to evaluate its proper place within the economy of the authentic life as it emerges from our reflection upon the Apollonian-Dionysian dialectic.

1. APOLLO AND DIONYSUS—TWO VIEWS OF AUTHENTIC LIFE

THE APOLLONIAN WAY[2]

Apollo is the god who most fully incarnates the ideals we associate with classical Greek thought. He is the god of ego, light, youth, purity, reasonableness, order, discipline, and balance. Perhaps the most characteristic maxim of the Apollonian way is the one that Socrates adopted (from the oracle at Delphi) as the basis of a philosophy of life—"Know thyself!" Know thyself to be a man, to be limited in time and space; above all, do not commit the folly of *hubris*—do not in pride presume to exceed the limits of mortality and aspire to the conditions of the gods.

Wisdom or authentic life in the Apollonian tradition consists of learning the rules and boundaries, and distinguishing with clarity between that which belongs to mortality and that which is immortal, between the knowable and the unknowable, the possible and the impossible, man and God, I and Thou, mine and yours. The happy man, having learned the proper limits of humanity, follows the way of moderation and seeks to govern the rebellious forces of the senses and the wayward imagination by the imposition of discipline. The human psyche is a commonwealth which the wise man will subject to the rule of reason. One might well see in Plato's figure of the Demiurge one model for the Apollonian view of man. Like the architect of the universe, man also must be a craftsman, a fabricator (*homo faber*) who grasps (or invents, in the case of the modern Apollonian thinker) the ideal and, by force of will, imposes it upon the recalcitrant and chaotic givenness of life. Man shares with the gods the responsibility for creating a cosmos in which reason and order prevail. The rule of law is the path of wisdom. Man must distinguish between the good and the evil, the permissible and the impermissible, and then, as a citizen in a commonwealth under law, take the responsibility for tailoring his inner and outer life to conform to what is required— to the laws governing nature, society, the psyche, and the relationship between God and man. Whatever impulses, desires, or actions run counter to the order necessary to a harmonious commonwealth must be repressed.

The Apollonian way has come to dominate the culture created by *homo faber*. Science and technology rest upon distinguishing clarifying, and gaining controlling knowledge over the environment. The world of science is the realm of law and regularity, where personal desires and impulses are disciplined and brought into conformity with the objective and verifiable modes of thought of the scientific community. Western political and psychological organization also tends to stress private property, individual responsibility, and the unique identity of the individual. We have come to see man as an atom living in a society of atoms, cut off from both the natural order below and the "supernatural" order above. The Apollonian organization of modern life is visible as one flies across the United States or any Western country. Where man is, order is obvious. The geometric patterns we impose on our fields and cities reveal our passion for neat boundaries—for the discipline of ownership and for distinguishing between my possessions and yours. Our laws which stress individual responsibility and guilt show that we organize psychic space in the same way as we structure physical space. Guilt before the law implies that one is in full possession of the personal faculties that make for responsibility.

THE DIONYSIAN WAY

Dionysus was a strange and wild god, an import both to the Greek countryside and the Greek spirit. He seems to have originated in Thrace, where he was a god of fertility and the energy of nature. On Greek soil he became associated with wine as well as with the metamorphosis which is symbolized in the cycle of the seasons. The worship of Dionysus was literally enthusiastic; it involved ecstasy, license, revelry, and direct participation, by eating, in the life of the dying and reborn god. In the ecstasy induced by wine and dancing the worshipers lost their own personalities and were merged with Dionysus. Thus the boundaries separating man, nature, and the divine were erased.

The essence of the Dionysian way is that it dares the extremes, and hence leads to a form of consciousness which is alien to the law-abiding and mean-respecting character of the Apollonian mind. The Dionysian way exalts ecstasy over order, the id over the ego, being possessed over a possessive orientation, the creative chaos of freedom over the security of inherited patterns of social and psychological organization, and divine madness over repressed sanity. As Nietzsche pointed out in his study of the Apollonian and Dionysian types, Prometheus is the model of the Dionysian way. Prometheus transgressed the boundaries of pride (*hubris*) in stealing fire from the gods, and was therefore condemned to punishment. The hard lesson he teaches is that "Man's highest good must be bought with a crime and paid for by the flood of grief and suffering which the offended divinities visit upon the human race in its noble ambition."[3]

Both the Genesis myth and Freud's mythology teach the same lesson—man becomes man only by breaking the laws that would refuse him the personal knowledge of good and evil—only by "killing the father," the source of authority and power who would keep him forever in a state of childhood and dependence. Only in abolishing the law—in denying any authority that dictates what he must become—does man become free.

Wisdom in the Dionysian tradition consists of continuing openness to the diverse and sometimes contradictory streams that flow through the depths of man. Man is not a property whose boundaries must be guarded against the intrusion of chaos by the watchful eye of the ego and its symbolically masked agents, but he is a nexus (Whitehead), a field of awareness where all dimensions of reality converge. The boundaries are created by the possessive instinct and by the cultural ideologies that sacrifice vividness to security and ecstasy to order. In yielding to possession by the god, one is inhabited by a holy power which informs all life, and the boundaries are broken down between I and thou, man and nature, man and God, ego and id. The self exists by its mystical participation in the power of being which is in all things. Once the boundaries of the ego are broken, the self is understood not so much as a substance having its own resident source of power but as one focus of a universal power, taking, for the moment, the form of an individual man. Nietzsche has spoken of the Dionysian way as one in which the principle of individuation is lost.

Not only does the bond between man and man come to be forged once more by the magic of the Dionysiac rite, but nature itself, long alienated or subjugated, rises again to celebrate the reconciliation with her prodigal son, man. The earth offers its gifts voluntarily, and the savage beasts of the mountain and desert approach in peace . . . . Now the slave emerges as a free man; all the rigid, hostile walls which either necessity or despotism has erected between men are shattered. Now that the gospel of universal harmony is sounded, each individual becomes not only reconciled to his fellow but actually at one with him—as though the veil of Maya had been torn apart and there remained only shreds floating before the vision of mystical Oneness. Man now expresses himself through song and dance as the member of a higher community; he has forgotten how to walk, how to speak, and is on the brink of taking wings as he dances.

Each of his gestures betokens enchantment; through him sounds a supernatural power, the same power which makes the animals speak and the earth render up milk and honey. He feels himself to be god-like and strides with the same elation and ecstasy as the gods he has seen in his dreams. No longer the *artist,* he has himself become *a work of art;* the productive power of the whole universe is now manifest in his transport, to the glorious satisfaction of the primordial One . . . .[4]

This loss of individuality which is at the heart of the Dionysian way has been expressed by modern thinkers in diverse terminology. Heidegger makes a complete analysis of the human condition without using the word "man." Man becomes *Dasein,* "being there," an instance of Being, not a hermetic substance with an autonomous power of being. Norman Brown understands authentic life as requiring the death of the ego and a passivity by which *we are lived,* inhabited. Alan Watts, drawing on the insights of Zen and Eastern mysticism, makes substantially the same point as Brown. The authentic life, which Buddhism has spoken of as *nirvana,* involves losing the illusion of the ego as a separate agent.

Nirvana is a radical transformation of how it feels to be alive: it feels as if everything were myself, or as if everything—including "my" thoughts and actions—were happening of itself. There are still efforts, choices, and decisions, but not in the sense that "I *make* them"; they arise of themselves in relation to circumstances.[5]

If the more characteristic models for the Apollonian way are the activities of fabrication (God making the world in conformity with his *logos,* man making himself in the image of some ideal) and legislation (God and man projecting laws which hold chaos in check and allow community), the model for the Dionysian way is the dance. Life is flux, movement, a dynamic power which assumes form for a moment and then changes. There is no end-point, no complete product. In the strict sense of the word there can be no integrity (a state of being complete, whole, unbroken) of individual life. Everything is a fraction, incomplete without its counterpart. In the dance of life, male and female, work and play, creativity and fallowness, day and night, and life and death belong together in a *rhythmic* unity. Identity is in movement; it lies in the interplay of the fractions that create a community in diversity. Authentic thought is, as Nietzsche said, thought that dances. Kazantzakis' figure of *Zorba the Greek* might well be taken as a concrete illustration of the Dionysian way and of the centrality of dance as an organizing metaphor for life. Zorba dances when the joy or the tragedy of life overflows the capacity of his words.

Two other metaphors are also frequently used to characterize the Dionysian way—fire and war. Fire is always moving and consuming what it touches; life is not being but becoming, not substance but process, as Heraclitus said at the beginning of Western philosophy and as Hegel and Whitehead have reminded us more recently. Dionysian life is also war, because in the flux of experience the opposites belong together. Life is dialectic; hence, thesis and antithesis are bound together in conflict. True warfare—like sex, and like contest (agon)—requires friendly enemies; it requires love of the enemy. Human communication at its best is, as Jaspers has said, "loving combat." We wrestle together in dialogue (which is polite warfare) in order that the whole truth may emerge from the incomplete and fractured individual perspectives.

The Dionysian way is one of iconoclasm and breaking down the walls. In destroying the traditional boundaries and limits that inform our accepted notions of personality and society, the Dionysian way flirts with madness. As psychoanalysis has demonstrated, there is at the depths of every person a wilderness—a chaos never domesticated by the "identity" we assume or the "personality" we put on "to meet the faces that we meet." The Dionysian wisdom is that we must immerse ourselves in this wilderness, which we usually repress and know only in dreams and daydreams (both brief psychotic episodes) and in the cultivated symbols of art and religion. The source of the power for vivid life lies locked in the unconscious. To be vital we must risk madness, as Zorba the Greek points out in his criticism of the life-style of his Appollonian "boss":

"No, you're not free," he said. "The string you're tied to is perhaps longer than other people's. That's all. You're on a longer piece of string, boss; you come and go, and think you're free, but you never cut the string in two . . . . It's difficult, boss, very difficult. You need a touch of folly to do that; folly, d'you see? You have to risk everything! But you've got such a strong head, it'll always get the better of you. A man's head is like a grocer; it keeps accounts: I've paid so much and earned so much and that means a profit of this much or a loss of that much! The head's a careful little shopkeeper; it never risks all it has, always keeps something in reserve. It never breaks the string. Ah no! It hangs on tight to it, the bastard! If the string slips out of its grasp, the head, poor devil, is lost, finished! But if a man doesn't break the string, tell me, what flavor is left in life? The flavor of camomile, weak camomile tea? Nothing like rum—that makes you see life inside out!"6

CONFLICT BETWEEN APOLLO AND DIONYSUS

The conflict between the Apollonian and the Dionysian styles of life is perennial.

Classical Greek culture was so pervaded by reverence for the Apollonian ideal of moderation that it viewed Dionysus as the source of tragedy. In a play like *The Bacchae* by Euripides we see a warning issued against Dionysus: emotion must not overcome reason; vitality must remain within the boundaries of accepted social forms; In philosophy as well as the tragic drama we find the ideal of an integrated rule of reason in which the individual, the polis, and the cosmos are equally governed by a *logos* which keeps all things from overstepping their boundaries. All chaos that threatens the divine order of reason is highly suspect. Apollo warns us that enthusiasm destroys those who yield to it and advises that it is better to observe the rule of reason than to risk ecstasy and chaos. Gradually Greek culture saw the necessity for a moderate worship of Dionysus and gave him a place of honor alongside Apollo at Delphi. Wonder and ecstasy are of value if they are placed within the context of a well-ordered life. However, on the metaphysical level Apollo remained the god of the Greeks and finally led them into a prison of cosmic fatedness in which spontaneity and freedom were destroyed by the lawfulness of fate.

At this point Christianity emerged as the advocate of Dionysus. Christianity came into the ancient world as a rebellion against the stifling domination of Apollo. It fought, on the one hand, against the Greek notion that history was ruled by the iron law of fate, and on the other hand against the Hebraic idea that life should be structured in conformity to religious and ceremonial laws. The good news proclaimed: law is not omnipotent either in the physical or the moral universe; novelty can happen in history; love is ontologically more fundamental than law, and therefore the authentic man is free from cosmic and moral legalism. Christianity saw tragedy as resulting from any formalism, legalism, or determinism which prevented the divine power that grants ecstasy, freedom, and novelty from invading life. Men need saving from the law—from Apollo. It must be confessed, with some sadness, that as Christian culture developed in the West it did not remain true to its Dionysian origins. It soon produced a new legalism, traditionalism, and orthodoxy which itself forbade novelty. No new epiphany could occur, because Christ was the definitive intrusion of the divine into history, and thus the Christian community lived by remembrance of things past and hope for things to come, but with little expectation that any present moment was radically open to the divine.

In the contemporary scene the Dionysian ideal is deeply ingrained in American ideology. The notion that America is a wonder-land, an historical experiment in which radical novelty is possible, permeates our self-understanding. The political rhetoric which has informed the American consciousness stresses the discontinuity between the old world and the new. In Europe, history, tradition, and the dead hand of the past may prohibit novelty from emerging, but the New World belongs to the present and the future rather than the past, and to freedom rather than servitude. A number of literary critics have recently observed that the charracteristic theme of the American novelist has been recovery of innocence and wonder. Until the disillusionment of the American intellectual following World War I, the American myth stressed the possibility of a new beginning, a rebirth of wonder. Tony Tanner, in an excellent book on American literature, *The Reign of Wonder*, has shown that the American writer has consistently sought a naïveté of response and perception which often involved him in a lasting interest in the child. More than the European writer, he has sought a wondering vision, an innocent eye, uninfluenced by the accretion of tradition. America is the new land, the wonder-land where the new Adam, like Huck Finn, can see the world without blinders or distortion. Like Ferlinghetti, most American writers have been "perpetually awaiting a rebirth of wonder." This ideology has also been preserved in popular folk tradition and continues to dominate the mythology of the Western movie. Television and the film industry find nothing so certain of success as the story of the archetypal hero who struggles westward to seek a new life free from the power structure of the old world and the mistakes of the past. On the far side of the Alleghenies there is a new beginning, where the hero is judged only by what he can do and never by where he has come from.

It is sometimes said that America is losing both its romantic "illusions" and its spiritual heritage. The process of intellectual aging has taken over; fat has grown upon our spirits and we have ceased to be a wonder-land where a man may discard the blinders of history and tradition and see with the eye of innocence. While it may be that security rather than adventure, familiarity rather than novelty, and satiety rather than innocent anticipation have come to characterize the dominant American style of life and politics, there is a resilience in the romantic hope and quest for the recovery of wonder. Novelty, ecstasy, and wonder may be banished from a society for a period, but Dionysus reasserts himself as surely as spring returns. Perhaps the most dramatic reassertion of the perennial American quest for wonder-land is in the emerging Dionysian revolution.

The contemporary Dionysian revolution has three foci. (1) Intellectuals such as Norman Brown, Herbert Marcuse, and Tom Altizer are arguing that Western culture has become repressively Apollonian—oriented toward ego, possession, security, and order at the expense of all that is delightful, erotic, playful, and innocent in man. They further argue that we now have sufficient knowledge of psychology and technology to allow a reorientation of life. The new man they see emerging will have a Dionysian consciousness; he will be a player rather than a worker and an enjoyer rather than an accumulator. (2) The "hippie" movement acts as if it had read and decided to practice the philosophy of Brown and Marcuse. They have dropped out of "straight" society and have begun to live by other values. However shocking or inane "flower power," "love-ins," and "blowing the mind" may seem, they reflect a quest that is typically American. The hippies want to know for themselves what life is about, and they reject the authority of any tradition which would settle the matter of values a priori. In urban

Waldens they force life into a corner and gaze at it with minds and senses oblivious to time. "Dropping out" and the use of hallucinogenic drugs are, among the hippies, an effort to cut through the accumulated residue of inherited modes of perception and action and go directly to experience of the primal simplicities of life. (3) The politicians of the new left share with other Dionysian thinkers the faith that the political, economic, and social order of contemporary society is destructive of the possibility of an open and just society. We must be prepared, therefore, to endure a period of chaos if a nonrepressive social order is to emerge. We shall further consider the emerging Dionysian revolution later in this chapter. For the moment it suffices to remind ourselves that the quest for the recovery of wonder is still viewed as essential to authentic life.

The Apollonian ideal is also an ineradicable aspect of contemporary ideology. We have already found that *homo faber,* a basically Apollonian model of man, is *the* characteristic contemporary model of man. American pragmatism creates an atmosphere in which enthusiasm is highly suspect. It views the authentic life as being rooted in action rather than contemplation. Consciousness is not viewed as a way of seeing (contemplating-wondering-theorizing) but as a way of acting on the environment. Thus, man relates to the world as one who asks questions, poses problems, and seeks solutions. The passive mode of wondering appreciation bakes no bread. With some truth it has been suggested that in America one could make a good living translating poetry into prose! The pragmatic mind is profoundly uncomfortable in the presence of any phenomenon where the appropriate course of action is not obvious. It must constantly ask: What shall I do about it—how can I change the situation?

EVALUATION OF MODELS

The perennial conflict between the Apollonian and the Dionysian models of authentic life raises the question of how we are to evaluate the adequacy of competing models of man. While we recognize that any model is an artificial construct which clarifies by exaggeration, and no concrete person or culture interprets existence or forms identity exclusively in relation to one model, we must nevertheless find a method for evaluating the adequacy of models having different emphases. It is only by determining the limitations of different models that we can see how basic attitudes such as wonder fit within the economy of the healthy personality. The method we shall use to test adequacy is that of *radicalization*. What happens when one model of man is used too exclusively—when either Apollo or Dionysus asumes nearly absolute control of personality? This method involves a study of the philosophical and psychological imbalance characteristic of different styles of illness. The search for an adequate model of authentic life will thus proceed by examining the logic of pathology. If we can discover the logic of different styles of illness we can isolate some of the principles of healthy life.

We should note in passing that while any given individual may major in one style of life or style of illness, he is not precluded from having elements of the opposite style. Pure types exist only as logical constructs. Indeed, in most forms of psychopathology we find an oscillation between Apollonian and Dionysian moments —between feelings of capitivity-limitation-impotence and feelings of grandiosity-limitlessness-omnipotence. *Our study of pathology is thus an effort to clarify the logic of the different (1) moments and (2) styles of illness.*

It should be clear that we are introducing an odd but, hopefully, interesting notion of the indivisibility of illness. We are accustomed to thinking about physical and mental illness, but usually we do not apply the term pathology to philosophical world views and models of man. It is part of the antimetaphysical bias of our age to assume that the way we view the ultimate context of human existence has nothing to do with sickness or health. Sickness results from germs, malfunctioning organs, disturbed human relationships, and possibly from political and social chaos, but not from mistaken or unbalanced philosophical ideas. My proposal is that pathology is indivisible; it has psychic, social, and philosophical (affective, behavioral, and cognitive) dimensions. Since man is that creature who constructs world views and models of himself, an unbalanced philosophy no less than disturbed personal relationships or inappropriate feelings is a symptom of illness. Therefore we must speak of *ideopathology* no less than psychopathology and sociopathology (the view that societies may be sick—e.g., Nazi Germany—not to be confused with the individual illness formerly referred to as psychopathic personality).

We may get a clue as to how we can diagnose ideopathology by asking the question of function. How does a given model of man function? What attitudes, feelings, actions, and aspirations does it render appropriate? If a philosophical model encourages attitudes and actions which, if consistently followed, would result in what we would clearly label inappropriate, unbalanced, and destructive, we may rightly suspect that we are dealing with an ideopathic philosophy. If, for instance, two different language systems both function in a similar manner to destroy confidence in the potency of human freedom, they are equally pathological; although one may use the intimate and personal vocabulary of biography while the other uses the universal, abstract categories of philosophy. The world view of a compulsive neurotic who must yield to the necessity of washing his hands after every contact with another person is different only in degree from that of the Marxist who lives under the illusion that his every action is governed by the necessary laws of historical dialectic. If the category of necessity is all-pervasive, it matters little whether the power supposed to govern human existence is located in the stars, the psyche, the will of God, or the laws of matter or society. In all of these cases human responsibility will be denied to some degree and the full range of human possibility will never be explored.

I do not raise here the question of cause and effect. It is, perhaps, impossible to determine with accuracy the exact relationship between the physical energy and psychic strength necessary for vivid existence, and social systems and philosophical models. At the very least, we must posit a reciprocal relationship between feeling, action, environment, and philosophical models of authentic life. Our task here is to trace the logic of illness and health (pathology and hygiology) by determining the point at which the Apollonian and Dionysian modes of life each becomes destructive of the balance and economy essential to health. While I maintain that pathology is ultimately indivisible, I shall for the sake of convenience refer to psychopathology as the study of the affective and volitional elements of illness, and to ideopathology as the study of the cognitive aspects of the inauthentic or unbalanced person. Since ours is primarily a study in models of self-understanding, we shall not deal in any systematic manner with sociopathology, although it may well be that the political and economic dimensions of the current crisis in identity are the dominant causal factors.

2. A TYPOLOGY OF MOMENTS AND STYLES OF PATHOLOGY

APOLLONIAN PATHOLOGY

A dominantly Apollonian style of life remains authentic and healthy only so long as it integrates some of the virtues of freedom and spontaneity that characterize the Dionysian way. As a working definition we may say that the Apollonian style of life becomes pathological when the vision of the necessary destroys the vision of the possible—when law denies novelty, when reason eclipses enthusiasm, when compulsion prevents spontaneity, or when the regular ceases to be wonderful.

Psychopathology

Apollonian psychopathology may be viewed as a continuum, ranging from the occasional fantasies and feelings of depression and captivity of the normal person to the depersonalized world of the psychotic which is under the total command of a hierarchy of projected private gods or demons. We shall make use of the idea of a continuum to locate the differing degrees of the experience of captivity. I do not mean to suggest that any given individual will necessarily progress along the continuum. Indeed, strangely enough, it frequently happens that a mild form of illness seems to innoculate the sufferer against a more severe form of the same illness; neurosis is often a protection against psychosis.

We may begin at the level of fantasies and dreams which seem to be common among normally functioning persons. One of the archetypal dreams of terror poses a situation in which we find ourselves either constricted in a space which is too narrow to permit movement or being chased by an animal or a dangerous person from whom we cannot escape. The experience of space in such dreams may serve as a small-scale model of the pathological experience of necessity and captivity. In claustrophobic dreams the space in which one is forced to live is too narrow and repressive for comfortable existence; it lacks openness and hence produces a feeling of stifling limitation. In a similar manner, in those dreams where one is unable to escape from impending danger, the body is experienced as rooted and trapped in its living space. We enter more deeply into the world of pathology as feelings such as these become more intense and the total psychic space is experienced as oppressive and closed.

Moving a slight distance on the continuum, we find the phenomenon of depression or melancholia. The literal meaning of depression suggests the emotional similarity between dreams of captivity and the feeling of being pressed down or heavily weighted and unable to move with grace or freedom. In depression a limited openness or freedom remains. A depressed person may continue to function socially, but he exists in a world lacking buoyancy, joy, or expectation. His life consists of feelingless repetition of routine acts. At best, he is a Sisyphus—tied to a meaningless burden, to an endless repetition of a fated action, a nihilistic ritual. (The phenomenon of depression raises questions about Camus' optimistic belief that Sisyphus is joyful as he returns to the bottom of the hill to roll the stone up again.) One patient described his experience of depression in these terms: "I seem shut into myself, withdrawn from real contact with the outer world as also from contact with God; the sun does not really shine, the trees and fields are not really green; I am shut in with my thoughts, always of a depressing and melancholy nature . . . ."[7]

In depression there is neither hope nor vividness of perception; wonder and enjoyment are both banished, and there remains only interior emptiness and poverty filled with vague sorrows, fears, and a diffuse sense of despair.

The psyche, however, abhors a vacuum. Hence, as depression deepens, obsessions and compulsions rush in to fill the void. Rather than face what one patient called "the pit of insecurity beneath the surface of life,"[8] the depressed individual may gradually become emotionally and intellectually convinced that he is in the power of an alien force or law. He may feel a compulsion to wash after every contact with the contaminated world, or he may suddenly become captive of recurring irrational fears that he will kill some-one he loves. Better to be a victim than a vacuum; better to be in bondage to the necessity of an inner compulsion than face the void of emotional emptiness! The relation between compulsion and con-striction of the openness of lived space is illustrated in the follow-ing incident from the case history of a compulsive patient.

If one of these (neighborhood) people touched me, I would have to wash the affected garment with soap flakes or benzine. Or someone who had been there (the cemetery) would come to our house, and then I cannot move around properly. I have the feeling as if the rooms were becoming too narrow and I were hitting everything with my dress. I have to go through the door sideways. In order to find peace, I wash everything in soapy water .and, depending on the circum-stances, I also have to wash the dress which I wore at the time. Then everything becomes large and wide again and I have room . . . .[9]

Here we have illustrated on an intimate biographical level the manner in which a rigid system of behavior, a life-style of obedi-ence to inner necessity, is constructed. By adherence to a compul-sive ritual of washing, the world is decontaminated and "every-thing becomes large and wide again." Obedience to the letter of the inner law is the price that must be paid to escape the narrow place where life is threatened.

At the far end of the continuum of the Apollonian style of pa-thology is the type of schizophrenia (paranoid) in which a fantasy kingdom is constructed which is inhabited by a hierarchy of au-thorities, demons, and gods, who conspire to create a world of total compulsion. Hannah Green has described one such kingdom with great penetration in *I Never Promised You a Rose Garden.* We find another classic example in Bruno Bettelheim's report of Joey, "the mechanical boy." Joey fantasied himself a machine and acted as if he were operated by remote control. He would string an imaginary wire from his "energy source" and acted as if he would die if the wires were disconnected.

Many times a day he would turn himself on and shift noisily through a sequence of higher and higher gears until he "exploded," screaming "Crash, crash!" and hurling items from his ever present apparatus—

radio tubes, light bulbs, even motors or, lacking these, any handy breakable object. (Joey had an astonishing knack for snatching bulbs and tubes unobserved.) As soon as the object thrown had shattered, he would cease his screaming and wild jumping and retire to mute, motionless nonexistence.[10]

In such examples, conduct becomes coerced or automatic, and the individual is an arena in which alien forces compete rather than an agent who has control over himself. Bettelheim says of Joey, "In Joey's machine world everything, on pain of distant destruction, obeyed inhibitory laws much more stringent than those of physics . . . . In his moments of silent withdrawal, with his machine switched off, Joey was absorbed in pondering the compulsive laws of his private Universe."[11]

The limiting laws, necessities, oughts, and powers which govern the inner world of psychopathology are defined on the small scale of individual biography. The rituals of captivity which each neurotic or psychotic develops and the inner laws to which he must be obedient—the gods and demons who dictate all his feelings, actions, and obligations—are constructed of the materials of private imagination. The limits are rigidly set by introjected authorities before whose eyes the victim is pathetically small and impotent.

Ideopathology

In what we are calling ideopathology, the world is experienced as totally governed by necessity and law, but the language of necessity is not personal and biographical. It is categorical, universal, and abstract.

Philosophies of life—whether individual or political, formal or informal, aristocratic or vernacular—reflect a pathological orientation to life whenever they conspire to destroy wonder and freedom by picturing the world as a closed system which may be understood and explained without remainder. While Apollonian pathology may masquerade in the diverse languages of metaphysics, science, politics, or common sense, it is always an outgrowth of the conspiracy to deny novelty, wonder, and freedom. Each closed system is a way of explaining that what seems to be novel and wonderful is, upon closer examination, merely necessary, natural, or ordinary. In order to evade the threat (and the promise) of novelty and freedom, the individual is insulated from the shock of strangeness by an ideology which creates the illusion of necessity. When novelty threatens to intrude, it is politely ushered into a pigeonhole which has been prepared in advance; it is placed within an a priori scheme of explanation, or in a holding area marked: "For recalcitrant facts and experiences which cannot yet be integrated into accepted patterns of thought." In each case the assumption is that there is an impersonal law to which man must submit: reality consists of chains of cause and effect or stimulus and response. Apollonian pathology reduces the personal to the impersonal; it understands the individual only as an instance of a general law; it limits freedom to the subjective acceptance of an already programed necessity; it equates wonder with a temporary state of curiosity which is caused by ignorance of adequate explanation.

Let us look at some examples from a wide variety of seemingly different philosophies of life: the idealism of Hegel, the materialism of Marx, scientism, and common sense.

The aristocrat of philosophical visions of necessity is the idealistic system of Hegel. Hegel's thought is built upon the principles of rational, as opposed to causal, explanation. Causal explanation is unsatisfactory, because it is mere formalized observation which does not explain anything. The effect does not resemble the cause, hence does not explain it. In order to explain the world the first principle of philosophy must be reason rather than cause. Only a world governed by rational necessity allows us to see why things are, and must be, as they are. Absolute Mind or Spirit is the first principle from which all may be deduced. Thus, in theory, Hegel's thought banishes all mystery from the world. The mysterious is merely the historical residue of the irrational which has not yet been conquered by Spirit. The rational is the real, and the historical process is the incarnation of the movement of reason. The enlightened man can see that all is necessity; all happens as it must, and there is, therefore, no real tragedy or contradiction in history.

Kierkegaard, in his polemic against Hegel, gave the classical arguments against any closed system of thought. There is no perspective that man can occupy from which the category of necessity may be seen to apply to existence. From the perspective of God or Absolute Spirit it may, or may not, be the case that all is necessary—that what is, is what ought to be. At any rate, man is a limited historical being who arrives at his portion of truth only by free decision and the leap of faith. In criticism of Hegel, Kierkegaard writes,

> If the philosopher never finds occasion to wonder (and how could it occur to anyone to wonder at a necessary construction, except by a new kind of contradiction?) he has *eo ipso* nothing to do with the historical; for wherever the process of becoming is involved, as is the case in relation to the past, there the uncertainty attaching to the most certain of events (the uncertainty of becoming) can find expression only in this passion, which is as necessary to the philosopher as it is worthy of him.[12]

According to Kierkegaard, if human beings avoid pride (which made Hegel pretend to view history from the perspective of the Absolute) and remain true to the limits of historical existence, they discover that a balance of freedom and destiny or possibility and necessity is required for authentic life.

With Karl Marx, the philosophical vision of necessity becomes materialistic, political, and vernacular. Marx turns the idealistic philosophy of Hegel on its head; he discovers the necessity that rules history in matter rather than Spirit. Matter is composed of the clash of moving particles just as societies are composed of the warring interests of different classes. There is an inevitable logic of history which shapes social institutions and ideologies, and which will eventually culminate in the overthrow of the exploiting class and the dictatorship of the proletariat. History moves with necessity, hence the individual is swept along and his only choice is whether to enter joyfully into the inevitable revolution or to succumb reluctantly. Freedom, in Marxist philosophy as in Stoicism, is reduced to graceful acquiescence to what must be. Epictetus' hymn to Zeus need only have the word "Zeus" replaced with "Historical Inevitability" to provide a Marxist creed:

> Lead me, O Zeus, and thou O Destiny,
> The way that I am bid by you to go;
> To follow I am ready. If I choose not,
> I make myself a wretch, and still must follow.
> But whoso nobly yields unto necessity,
> We hold him wise, and skill'd in things divine.[13]

Both the idealism of Hegel and the materialism of Marx seem strangely old-fashioned in the twentieth century. The contemporary philosophies of necessity are pragmatic rather than theoretical— operational and methodological rather than systematic. Our century has been marked by a revolt against formal philosophical and metaphysical systems. With systematic philosophy in disrepute, we have turned our concern to epistemology, methodology, and "styles of life."

Foremost among the pseudo-philosophical methods of excluding novelty and handing the world over to the total rule of law is the phenomenon variously called positivism, scientism, or reductionism, upon which I have previously commented. There are two characteristics which all modes of positivism and scientism share and which show marked similarity to psychopathological states. First, positivism shares with neurosis the demand for 100-per-cent certainty. The neurotic asks for moral perfection or absolute certainty that his course of action will be successful before making a decision; the positivist requires public verification of all knowledge claims, that is, cognitive certainty. The existentialist insight (which insists that there are modes of *knowledge* which require risk, commitment, willing, feeling, and desiring) is denied a priori by the positivist. No subjective, "emotional" certainty can provide a basis for responsible knowledge claims. Only the publicly verifiable, the repeatable—that which conforms to universal law—can be dignified by the title "knowledge." Such a demand for absolute cognitive certainty leads to the second characteristic. Since valid understanding must be publically verifiable, the explanation of any event or object is reduced to a conceptual scheme which may become the mental possession of any observer. Explanation, in positivism, becomes reductionism. A thing is reduced to the manageable. A bird song becomes only a specific instance of the general phenomenon of the protection of territory; a state of oceanic feeling becomes a chemical phenomenon. The unique dimension of a person, thing, or event which can be known only within what Buber called a loving encounter cannot be fitted into positivist modes of explanation. Marcel has noted that whenever we find ourselves using the formula: this is *only* a ——— (projection, feeling, Communist tactic, etc.) we are in danger of using explanation as an exorcism of those dimensions of meaning which escape the net of our abstractions. "Every depreciatory reduction of this sort has its basis in resentment, that is to say, in a passion, and at bottom it corresponds to a violent attack directed against a sort of integrity of the real, an integrity to which only a resolutely concrete mode of thinking can hope to do justice."[14]

The parallel with neurosis is obvious here. The neurotic allows only those persons, ideas, and feelings into his world which can be manipulated to suit his ends (whether the mode of manipulation be active or passive), and he refuses to perceive those dimensions of reality which are irrelevant to his manipulative intent. The positivist exorcises those dimensions which cannot be possessed with absolute certainty. This denial of the intrinsic reality of what escapes controlling knowledge roots in the desire to debunk and exorcise the mystery which can be encountered but not possessed.

A final example of philosophical pathology is the conviction that "common sense" and social convention provide the only infallible norms of knowledge and conduct. If we take vivid awareness of the possibility of novelty as one criterion of authentic life, we cannot evade the conclusion that there is a pathology of normality. The "average" or "normal" individual takes his clues from the accepted attitudes of his social context; common sense informs him that what "everybody" says must be true and what "everybody" does must be right. Thus, if the government commits atrocities against civilian populations and justifies it as necessary to bring lasting peace and dignity to the world, the average person assumes "they" (government is always conducted by an anonymous "they") must be acting morally and wisely. The average man has surrendered his perception and judgment to the mass; what he judges as beautiful or ugly, moral or immoral, or possible or impossible is a mere ratification of the lowest common denominator of socially accepted attitudes and convictions. In this pathology of conformism the law or necessity which prevents the intrusion of novelty is the unexamined value system of the mass. The highest condemnation of an act becomes the ancient cry, "Such a thing is not done in Israel!" The imperatives of the mass require obedience which is unquestioning; the authority of the mass invites no rational inquiry and no reflection upon the necessities it imposes. The motto of the pathology of normality is: "Always prefer the known over the unknown and tradition over innovation," or, as the English proverb has it: "Always keep a hold on nurse for fear of meeting something worse."

Results of Apollonian Pathology

We have seen a basic structural similarity between certain compulsive and paranoid states of mental illness and various deterministic philosophies of life. It remains to show that wherever the category of necessity reigns supreme (whether the language in which it is expressed be psychological, theological, philosophical, or social), there results a shriveling of life, which is accompanied by a distortion of the capacity to wonder.

In the broadest terms, the result of the Apollonian pathology is to turn the world into a prison. Instead of imposing sufficient law, order, and reason on the wilderness of chaos and contingency to render the world a home, the compulsive, the philosophical determinist, and the social conformist turn everything into obligation, necessity, or fate.

So long as the law-abiding and necessary character of the cosmos was experienced as mediating a transcendent purpose or presence, admiration remained. As we have seen, the rational character of reality was a cause for celebration for traditional man. Also, we must remember that the first fruit of natural science was a widened sense of wonder and admiration of the intricate mathematical order of the created world. The ordered workings of the eye and the heavens were to Newton positive evidence of the existence of a Divine Mathematician. By the middle of the nineteenth century, however, awareness of the awful lawfulness of all things began to give rise to a feeling of captivity in a morally neutral, causally determined universe. It would not be wide of the mark to suggest that much of the modern sense of despair and resentment, arising from the conviction that there is no escape from the necessity that governs things, closely resembles the attitudes of the ancient Gnostics, who felt the world to be the well-governed prison house of an alien deity. Where there is necessity but no purpose, order but no *logos*, or law but no Presence, admiration and wonder are replaced by attitudes appropriate to captivity.

When every present moment is the inevitable outcome of the past, the sense of astonishment and adventure are replaced by weariness, boredom, and finally despair. When there can be "nothing new under the sun," all turns into "vanity and striving after wind" and resentment against fate. Such cosmic captivity differs from neurosis only in the size of the prison and in the identity of the guards. Mothers, fathers, and repressive authorities guard the hermetic world of the neurotic, while the cosmic prison of the determinist is watched over by a neutral force which has no name or purpose. The neurotic at least has the hope of escaping from his captivity, because he can name and hence deal with his captors. The determinist can address his rebellion only to "it" or "they," and such messages are never acknowledged, returned, or answered.

Apollonian pathology also destroys the intuition (which lies at the heart of the experience of wonder) that finite existence, with all its limited and tragic character, is nevertheless a gift. *When all is necessary, the given is equivalent to the imposed, and man is not a recipient but a victim.* Whatever happens to the psychological or philosophical determinist is the result of the working of an anonymous law which does not swerve in the slightest to make room for that uniqueness which distinguishes A. J. Ayer from B. F. Skinner. The only source of uniqueness the determinist can credit is accident. Accidents happen; there are deviations from general laws, and mutations occur, but these result from an unpredictable and unexplainable failure of an otherwise universal order.

The isolation of regularities, the elaboration of laws, the determination of limits, arise out of man's effort to understand and have dominion over the world. Ironically, when the notion of law or necessity is superimposed over the whole of experience, the free subject who sets out to control the world is reduced to a determined object—he is destroyed by his own creation. Whenever the self is thought to be ruled by the same anonymous law that governs the world of objects, freedom is proclaimed to be an illusion. Man, who had hoped to control his world—to create novelty, to do a new thing—wakes up to find himself in a prison of necessity which he has constructed. Whether total necessity arises from neurotic compulsion, baptizing social conventions, de-

terministic philosophical systems which rule out novelty, or methodological imperialism, it results in the destruction of the delicate
balance required to maintain human freedom. Kierkegaard drew
a vivid picture of the fate of the determinist.

The determinist or the fatalist is in despair, and in despair he has lost
his self, because for him everything is necessary. He is like that king
who died of hunger because all his food was transformed into gold.
Personality is a synthesis of possibility and necessity. The condition
of its survival is therefore analogous to breathing (respiration), which
is an in and an a-spiration. The self of the determinist cannot breathe,
for it is impossible to breathe necessity alone, which taken pure and
simple suffocates the human self.[15]

The ethical and psychological corollary of the loss of freedom
because of the omnipotence of law is seen in legalism. Once a law
is set up and the only path to authentic existence is rigid obedience
to it, freedom, spontaneity, and even the ability to be obedient
are destroyed. The law is death, as St. Paul observed. The necessity of abiding by the letter of the law destroys the ability to adhere
to its spirit. A world in which all the limits are preprogramed
leaves no room for creative response, for the creation of novel
patterns. Freedom to create and act are possible only where there
exists a continuing openness and receptivity to the givenness of
life and a continuing movement toward transcending the given.
To neglect either to accept the limits of the given or to transcend
them by resolve and action is to destroy freedom.

Freedom, wonder, and hope form an inseparable cluster of attitudes, all of which are threatened by the rigid formalism of Apollonian pathology. If we may characterize wonder as openness to
novelty in the present and freedom as action undertaken in the
confidence that the self may create a new thing, then hope is the
conviction that the future, no less than the present, is open to
radical novelty. As Marcel has noted, hope is the radical refusal
to calculate the limits of the possible. Future possibility is not to
be defined by already known limits; the past does not exercise an
absolute tyranny over the future. In hope the affirmation is made,
or the assurance given, that there is the possibility of novelty,
renewal, and integrity in spite of the seemingly necessary conclu-

sion dictated by the law of cause and effect. Necessity may be the penultimate context of human life, but the ultimate context is possibility. Hope affirms that novelty is ontologically more fundamental than law and that therefore we should face the unknown future with wonder, expectancy, and the willingness to decide. Such hope is not available to the pathological Apollonian personality.

Despair is the appropriate and logical conclusion of the Apollonian style of pathology. We may define despair as the absence of a sense of possibility, arising out of a judgment, conscious or unconscious, that the limits of the real are already determined and known. This is the type of judgment that animates the philosophy of Camus, as is eloquently illustrated by his use of a passage from Pindar as an epigram at the beginning of *The Myth of Sisyphus:* "O my soul, do not aspire to immortal life, but exhaust the limits of the possible." While Sartre views the world as radically contingent, a world in which "anything can happen," as the hero of *Nausea* says, Camus' thought emerges from the conviction that the limits of the possible are fully known. Despair is the logical starting point for a lucid philosophy because the die is cast—the energies of the universe are limited, the laws fixed.

The absurd man thus catches sight of a burning and frigid, transparent and limited universe in which nothing is possible but everything is given, and beyond which all is collapse and nothingness. He can then decide to accept such a universe and draw from it his strength, his refusal to hope, and the unyielding evidence of a life without consolation.[16]

Despair, anguish, rebellion, keeping the absurd alive, and fighting the plague of inevitable evil without the consolation of ultimate victory become the marks of the authentic life wherever Apollonian reason leads to an unquestioning assumption that the categories by which we are to understand the future of man are identical with those we use in understanding his past.

No matter how admirable the artistry and courage of Camus, his philosophy comes dangerously close to glorifying a style of life which may be empirically demonstrated as leading to psychopathology. William Lynch has shown in *Images of Hope* that mental illness results directly from hopelessness and lack of a sense of the possible. Wishing, willing, and hoping are essential to sanity, and these attitudes are appropriate only where the future is open for novelty. Despair, far from leading to vivid appreciation of the sweet certainties of the earth and full exploitation of the range of finite possibilities, calls human freedom into question. Only where surprise is possible can freedom survive. Despair is a hermetic impulse which denies the appropriateness of openness toward the future. If the future can bring no radical novelty then lucid intelligence can only be painfully aware that the necessity that rules destiny is neutral to the human desire for new beginnings.

We may note in passing that the vernal religious impulse of man is a continuing rebellion against Apollonian pathology. The hermetic impulse, that tendency to seal oneself into a closed living space which is the essence of the Apollonian way, can only be shown to be inappropriate if the ultimate context of human history is one of open possibility. In the past the symbol "God" has been used to affirm the ontological priority of possibility over necessity, of novelty over repetition, and of grace over compulsion. If God exists, all things are possible, and hope and wonder are appropriate attitudes and not tender-minded illusions. The religious impulse is founded upon the conviction that there is a perspective from which the apparent rule of necessity and death may be inserted into a broader context of freedom and ultimate possibility. Perhaps the most valuable contribution of existential theology has been to demonstrate that positing this perspective is not the same as assuming that any human being can occupy it, even in imagination (which has been the mistake of idealism and religious orthodoxies). Agnosticism and hope are not incompatible.

DIONYSIAN PATHOLOGY

We may characterize Dionysian pathology as beginning when the vision of possibility destroys awarenes of the necessities and limits that govern existence as it is presently known. In Dionysian madness all limits, boundaries, and laws are dissolved in the endless flux of existence, and the world is reduced to chaos and absolute contingency. The world becomes a wilderness which cannot be domesticated by thought, will, or action. When enthusiasm is not tempered with judgment, man loses his rootedness in the limitations of the present, and he soars into the situationlessness of pretended omnipotence.

Psychopathology

The Dionysian style of psychopathology may also best be understood as a continuum ranging from fantasies of being without limits to psychotic delusions of omnipotence. In recounting the various steps in the continuum, we are tracing the logic of the deepening experience of the vacuity of the self living in a world that is increasingly terrible, contingent, and chaotic.

Let us begin with the fantasies and dreams of normal persons (remembering that every dream and fantasy is a momentary psychosis). The archetypal Dionysian terror may be found in dreams of falling, of being lost in a boundless space, or of coming apart at the center. In all such dreams, space is experienced as terrifyingly immense and empty. No necessity or gravity anchors the body and keeps it in the place where it belongs. The body has so little density or substance that it may be blown away by a wind or fall apart, because it lacks a center which can enforce cohesion and unity on its parts. In dreams of falling or being lost in a featureless desert, the space that surrounds the self cannot be domesticated; it is the space of a horizon of possibilities so vast and endless that a man may never locate himself within it. No law, no limit, no boundary, and no familiar and stable landmarks exist which can serve to orient the man lost in the boundless.

Proceeding a step along the continuum, we arrive at a condition which is fast coming to characterize the average man in modern Western society—the state of *anomie*.

The idea of *anomie* was advanced by Durkheim to characterize the state of normlessness in a group, but it may also refer to individuals who suffer from absence of an inner sense of boundaries, laws, norms, or limits. The psychic condition of the anomic individual is one of undifferentiated, diffuse, total possibility. He recognizes no inner limits, because he has made no de-cisions. Having given his existence no definite shape either by claiming the norms of society as his own or by rebelling against the limits imposed by social expectation and setting up the boundaries of his own moral universe, the anomic individual lacks the sense of density and location which is essential to selfhood. He does not dare to have strong feelings or definite goals; thus, he drifts through life in a dream, adjusting to the slight pressure exerted by the environment. Because the anomic individual conforms outwardly to the norms of society, he may appear to himself as a decisive person. He repeats accepted opinions, which he changes when the climate changes. Although he conforms without passion, his conformity at least keeps the inner vacuum from becoming so strong that the demons of neurotic compulsion can enter and set up an arbitrary rule. The worst the anomic person suffers is a constant sense of staleness and emptiness of existence. Lacking either passion or compulsion, he is subject to a pervasive sense of boredom. In this sad dialectic (oscillation between conformism and inner emptiness) we can identify both the Apollonian and Dionysian moments of pathology.

Perhaps the best analogy we can draw to the anomic man is the state of weightlessness which an astronaut experiences in outer space. In weightlessness the body floats in space, and it can find nothing to push against to establish its own sense of rootedness and location. It is decision that first creates the ontological density of human personality. Thus, by avoiding the painful self-limitation of decision the anomic man evades the stigma of definiteness which is the sign both of human greatness and human finitude. By avoiding decision, both being and nonbeing—life and death— are ignored.

The transition between the anomic individual and the neurotic is difficult to trace. Both are characterized by inner vacuity and lack of any appropriate sense of limits, boundaries, goals, and values which are passionately and responsibly affirmed. The Dionysian element in neurosis is to be located in the hidden maxim that governs neurotic feeling and action rather than in overt action. To the observer the aggressive, expansive neurotic may appear Dionysian, while the passive dependent neurotic type may appear excessively conscious of restrictive limitations. However, opposite styles of action may be animated by a common maxim. As I have suggested earlier, at the heart of all neurosis is the hidden search for omnipotence—the effort to actualize an idealized image of the self. The omnipotent, idealized self of the neurotic is a throwback to the self of childhood, when the ego was the center of the world and commanded in imagination a kingdom of absolute possibility. To long for the infantile is to long for omnipotence. For, to the child, the world is a sphere of magical possibility—step on a crack and you break your mother's back; think of a toad and you get a wart; wish for your fathers' death and you commit murder. In omnipotence, childhood, primary process thinking, or neurosis, there is no margin between the thought and the deed, desire and reality, the imagined and the real. The dependent neurotic may seek to achieve his wish through passive manipulation, while the domineering one seeks to work his magic through more direct manipulative methods, but both seek the same end: a world in which reality coincides with the demands of the ego (or id)—in which fantasy does not differ from actuality.

R. D. Laing has defined what has previously been called neurosis as the "schizoid personality." The schizoid is not psychotic, but he is alienated from his world and lacks any sense of ontological weight or meaning. He has so little sense of his own autonomy and power that he is constantly anxious about being swallowed up, absorbed, or smothered by others. Since the schizoid person experiences himself as having no innate being, he must receive his validation from without. He must be presented with his identity by being recognized in the eyes of others; thus, his personality is constructed by the introjected approving and disapproving eyes of parents and peers. To be is to appear to others; hence, being is appearance, performance, and role-playing.

The clue to the Dionysian element in the schizoid personality is in the evasion of decision and limitation. As long as the self is mere appearance and does not become embodied in the world of objective events and actions, it remains free but fantastic. All possibilities remain open, because the self has no ground to which it is committed. Having no home in the definite, the schizoid becomes free to live in the fantasied heaven of infinite possibility.

The self, being transcendent, empty, omnipotent, free in its own way, comes to be anybody in phantasy, and nobody in reality. This self is related primarily to objects of its own phantasies. Being so much a self-in-fantasy, it becomes eventually volatilized. In its dread of facing the commitment to the objective element, it sought to preserve its identity; but, no longer anchored to fact, to the conditioned and definitive, it comes to be in danger of losing what it was seeking above all to safeguard. Losing the conditioned, it loses its identity; losing reality, it loses its possibility of exercising effective freedom of choice in the world . . . .[17]

In the genuine schizophrenic the break with an appropriate sense of limits is greater than in the schizoid personality. Schizophrenia is Dionysus with scarcely a trace of Apollo, or vice versa. When primary process thinking reigns supreme, the dream cannot be separated from the world of waking, the inside cannot be distinguished from the outside, and fantasy cannot be differentiated from reality. As Cameron notes,

In some schizophrenic patients, regression revives situations in which there are virtually no ego or self boundaries. When this is so, projection is a very primitive process, and the delusions and hallucinations which develop only succeed in confusing external and internal reality, in much the same way that manifest dreams do. Things and events which should be experienced as internal seem to be external, or fluctuate between seeming internal and external. At the same time, because of fluctuating and permeable boundaries, parts of the external world seem to be internal, and parts of the self seem to be outside the self. It is probable that in patients who regress deeply, and do not improve, representatives of the self and of the external world, including somatic parts, swim in an almost undifferentiated objectless dream world . . . .[18]

The imagined omnipotence in schizophrenia may become complete, as with one patient who reported:

I feel so close to God, so inspired by His Spirit that in a sense I am God. I see the future, plan the Universe, save mankind, I am utterly and completely immortal; I am even male and female. The whole Universe, animate and inanimate, past, present, and future, is within me. All nature and life, all spirits, are co-operating and connected with me; all things are possible. I am in a sense identical with all spirits from God to Satan. I reconcile Good and Evil and create light, darkness, worlds, universes . . . .[19]

The loss of the self in pure, unlimited possibility is inevitable when primary process thinking comes to dominate the personality. Without the limits imposed by awareness of social situation and bodily incarnation in a given time and space, the self becomes a myrmidon which may become inhabited by alien personalities and impulses. Thus, the schizophrenic may be possessed by Napoleon or Jesus or the Devil, but in such possession there is not the ecstasy promised by Dionysus—only the tragic loss of self and the terror of being defenseless against the intrusion of alien persons and things.

Ideopathology

Philosophical advocates of the Dionysian way of life have recently come to defend a model of man in which authentic consciousness is closely akin to schizophrenic consciousness. The schizophrenic has become a hero. In looking at the philosophical advocacy of the Dionysian consciousness, we must seek to distinguish between that touch of madness which is the essence of wisdom and sanctity, and pure madness in which human responsibility and dignity are destroyed. To distinguish between divine and demonic madness is to discover when Dionysus is the god of grace and when he is the bringer of destruction and pathology.

Although there are a number of contemporary thinkers seeking to renew the Dionysian option (Thomas Altizer, Nikos Kazantzakis, Norman Mailer, Herbert Marcuse, Alan Watts, and to a lesser degree Heidegger, Marcel, Tillich, and Whitehead), we shall center our attention upon what is perhaps the most brilliant defense of the Dionysian consciousness to emerge—the work of Norman O. Brown.

Norman Brown begins his analysis, innocently enough, following psychoanalytic theory which links civilization to the repression of sexual desires which were unrepressed in childhood. Western civilization has replaced infantile delight in the body with the substitute satisfactions of work, possession, and genital sexuality. In childhood the total body is erotic, or in Freudian terminology, "polymorphously perverse"; it values pleasure and delight more highly than reality. The repression that society demands of us is accomplished by focusing all erotic feeling in the genitals, so that the rest of the body (time, energy, and imagination) may be harnassed to the serious tasks of *homo faber*—producing artifacts and making history. The civilization we have created is thoroughly Apollonian. It denies the instincts and provides only substitute,

symbolic satisfactions. Thus it creates a split within man in which
body moves against spirit with increasing repression, guilt, and
aggression.

When Brown moves from analysis to prescription of a way
beyond the current situation, he becomes apocalyptic. In the last
chapter of *Life Against Death* he proposes the creation of a
Dionysian consciousness which would be based upon a body ego
of the polymorphously perverse body. The Dionysian consciousness would be without repression, negation, or guilt; hence, it
would act to enhance erotic pleasure rather than being driven to
action by anxiety and the desire for possessions. The unrepressed
man would be free to live and to die because he would have overcome anxiety and guilt. He would also be free from obsession
with genital sexuality and would exist in a world which was totally
eroticised. Being oriented toward delight and play, he would lose
the money complex and would demand happiness rather than
power and use-value rather than exchange-value.

The project of mapping the outlines of the Dionysian consciousness is carried through in *Love's Body*. While the argument of
Life Against Death moved in a Dionysian direction, its style was
purely Apollonian. Somewhere between the books Norman Brown
became converted to the message he was preaching and created
a literary medium appropriate to a Dionysian argument. *Love's
Body* consists of aphorisms, quotations, and philosophical free
associations which are, nevertheless, organized with such rigorous
logic (the logic of poetic evidence) as to present the case for a
Dionysian consciousness with great force and clarity.

Brown's polemic is directed against the traditional notion of the
individual skin-encapsulated ego. He stands solidly against the
position maintained by ego-psychologists, who insist that the wise
and mature man is one whose ego boundaries are well established
and defined. The arbitrary boundaries we establish between self
and not-self, inside and outside, good and bad, mine and thine,
subject and object, are mere defense mechanisms which keep us
from life. The ego is not the principle of strength but a set of rigid
boundaries which keeps us from living in vital communion with the
real world. The normal consciousness of common sense is what
sets up the divisions between self and world, and hence is the

source of alienation and schizophrenia. "The real world, which is not the world of the reality principle, is the world where thoughts are omnipotent, where no distinction is drawn between wish and deed."[20]

The way out of the living death of ordinary ego consciousness is apocalypse—the breaking down of boundaries, walls, divisions, defense mechanisms, literal meanings, authorities, and permanent forms. We must give up the reality principle which insists upon false boundaries drawn between inside and outside, subject and object, real and imaginary, and physical and mental. The ego must go. "Dionysus, the mad god breaks down the boundaries; releases the prisoners; abolishes repression; and abolishes the *principium individuationis,* substituting for it the unity of man and the unity of man with nature."[21]

The key word in the style of life Brown is recommending is brokenness. Authentic life involves being broken open and remaining porous to the amazing intrusions of reality. "To be is to be vulnerable. The defense mechanisms, the character-armor, is to protect from life. Frailty alone is human; a broken, a ground-up (contrite) heart."[22]

It is not occasional openness that Brown is urging—a momentary letting down of the masks and roles that make up our egos. He will have nothing of regression in the service of a broader ego identity. Rather, he is advocating the end of personality and the ego. "Accept loss forever. To lose one's own soul. 'Satori, when the ego is broken, is not final victory but final defeat, the becoming like nothing.' Or no one; I'm a noun."[23]

The form of consciousness which is to replace ego consciousness is closely akin to schizophrenia.

Definitions are boundaries; schizophrenics pass beyond the reality-principle into a world of symbolic connections: "all things lost their definite boundaries, became iridescent with many-colored significances." Schizophrenics pass beyond ordinary language (the language of the reality principle) into a truer, more symbolic language. "I'm thousands, I'm an in-divide-you-all. I'm no un (i.e., nun, no-un, no one)." The language of *Finnegans Wake.* James Joyce and his daughter crazy Lucia, these two are one. The god is Dionysus, the mad truth.[24]

Out of the brokenness of normal consciousness arises the Dionysian consciousness, which is symbolic rather than literal, cosmic rather than individual. Like the consciousness of the child or the schizophrenic, the Dionysian consciousness includes everything. The world is the body of the enlightened man. "Symbolic consciousness, the erotic sense of reality, is a return to the principle of ancient animistic science, mystical participation, but now for the first time freely; instead of religion, poetry."[25]

Fire is the form of authentic life, because it lives by being consumed. The Dionysian consciousness thus lives in a state of constant revolution and creates only perishable forms. "A new order is, correctly speaking, one which is renewed hourly. Permanent revolution, then, and no permanent (reified-visible) structures issuing from contract, commitment, promise, will or will power, which are from the ego. Not voluntarism, but spontaneity, or grace; not the ego but the id."[26]

It is hard to know how to evaluate Brown's thesis. He tells us that the Dionysian way advocates exaggeration as the path to wisdom, and since he obviously has a sense of humor he realizes that his own work is an insult to common sense. At the risk of offering prosaic criticism of the poetic (picture a ballet master trying to give dancing instructions at a Dionysian orgy), I must suggest that Brown's prescription for the cure of a repressed, Apollonian society runs the danger of killing the patient with too much of a good medicine. We may have to introduce a touch of madness into common sense if celebration and dancing are to emerge, but we must take care to guard against the insanity that results from the destruction of all boundaries and norms. As Richard Rubenstein has demonstrated in *After Auschwitz,* the death camps were nothing more than the political conclusion of the experiment of the elimination of all moral norms. Madness must be in conversation with sanity, the id with the ego, or the result will be a frenzy of destruction rather than an ecstasy of self-transcendence.

One of the reasons it is difficult to evaluate Brown's proposal is because he does not offer us sufficient clues to allow us to construct a concrete portrait of a Dionysian man. We are left wondering what a person with a cosmic consciousness which no longer negated anything would do to occupy his time. Kazantzakis gave us a vivid portrait of his view of the Dionysian personality in *Zorba the Greek,* but Brown seems to suggest that playing with language, dancing with words and ideas (the resexualization of language), is more significant than kinesthetic awareness and play. Since Brown's suggestion is for the creation of a new form of consciousness, we must try to feel our way into this mode of perceiving the world. It would seem that much of the material coming from the psychedelic revolution is relevant to evaluating the Dionysian consciousness. Although there is a difference of degree in the change in consciousness induced by ingestion of mild hallucinogenics such as marihuana and hashish and stronger agents such as LSD, DMT, and mescaline, the psychedelic experience seems to qualify as pure Dionysian consciousness. LSD produces the polymorphously perverse body in short order with such intensity that even the desire to play with language is dissolved in the pleasure of immediate experience. It may help us, in evaluating Brown's proposal, to comment upon some aspects of the psychedelic experience.

The defining characteristic of that experience is the transcendence or obliteration of the boundaries of the quotidian. Depending upon the strength and dosage of the drug ingested, the distinct divisions between objects and moments in time become blurred. Things flow together, like the forces in Van Gogh's "Starry Night," and all of reality seems to dance. No longer do the static, the distinct, and the sharply outlined rule the world of experience. The flow of time becomes slow, or paralyzed, or nonexistent, as in the world of childhood ("Mommy's minutes are hours, Mommy's hours are days," etc.), and with time suspended an infinity may be devoted to the enjoyment of any sensation. It becomes possible to take a trip lasting for eons into the taste of bread and wine, or into a phrase of music, or a loved face. Nor do the normal boundaries between the senses remain unchanged; it is possible to see music, hear colors, and see smells.

The distortion of the normal sense of time and of the boundaries between the senses is a part of the more radical dissolving of the ego which takes place in the psychedelic experience. When the rider of self-consciousness falls away, leaving pure awareness, the

I or ego is left behind, as is the distinction between subject and object, inside and outside, or here and there. This loss of a sense of the distinctness and separateness of the experiencing self accounts for both the aesthetic and the religious aspects of psychedelic experience. A beautiful object like a rose may be intuited in pure wonder because there is no longer an "I" looking at myself looking at the rose. There is only consciousness which may penetrate and become one with anything upon which it falls. The self is reduced to a focused awareness of the objects, events, and sensations that flow ceaselessly in the moving mandala of reality. Ego transcendence is often reported in religious terms, especially by those persons who have some knowledge of Eastern religions: the one becomes caught up in the flow of the All; the alienation caused by the illusion of atomic selfhood is dispelled, and painful self-awareness gives way to the ecstasy of being included in a moving totality.

Another aspect of the psychedelic experience which leads us to believe it is a candidate for Brown's Dionysian consciousness is its erotic component. The popular press has, quite characteristically, played up the connection between LSD and sex. Since any sensual experience is heightened when psychedelics are used, it is only natural to suppose that sexuality would be also. However, this misses the point. Aside from the physical lethargy which usually accompanies the use of psychedelics, genital sexuality is often rendered superfluous because of the erotic character of the total experience. The whole dance and flow of reality is experienced as erotic—a candle, a flower, or the aroma of wine may produce a quality of ecstasy which had previously been experienced only in genital sexuality. Freed from the pressure and anxiety produced by the knowledge of time's ruthless march toward death, egoless awareness finds delight in all things. In eternity there is no need to discriminate; there is time to enjoy everything. And when sex is only one flower in a garden of delight it ceases to be clutched after; it ceases to be "the one green thing in a world of steel and calculation." Thus the emphasis of the press is both right and wrong. The psychedelics place one in a more erotic but a less genital world. Where there is much to wonder at, sex becomes a delight among delights. LSD doesn't take the pot of gold from under the tree of sex; it merely, like Rumpelstiltskin in the children's fairy tale, ties a scarf around every tree in the forest.

I have thus far reported only the positive aspects of the psychedelic experience. If this were the whole story we might conclude that the Dionysian consciousness is the path to heaven on earth. However, as the Greek tragedies made clear, Dionysus is a god of paradox. He brings both rapture and horror, both life and death. The reverse side of the ecstasy of self-transcendence and ego loss is the terror of losing all those values and delights that are a part of our rootedness in a particular time, place, and situation. The loss of boundaries promises the release from chains of limitation, but it threatens destruction of the treasures which the boundaries encompass and keep safe.

The terrifying aspects of the psychedelic experience have been frequently reported but are still inadequately understood in psychodynamic and philosophical terms. What in slang is referred to as "freaking out," and in psychological terms as the temporary psychosis resulting from panic under LSD, is an integral aspect of the psychedelic experience that some voyagers learn to handle and others do not. With the approach of ego loss there comes the temptation to hold on to the familiar boundaries—to stay in control. Since it is impossible with the stronger psychodelics to retain normal control of consciousness, panic results when one is unable to relax and go with the experience and enjoy the positive aspects of ego-transcendence. Where LSD is used under proper medical supervision, intensive training is given in relaxation and a supportive environment is created so that the voyager may trust the therapist and the setting when he can no longer control his responses. At best, however, the experience of ego loss is fraught with the possibility of terror. Nor is this terror always a lack of courage to die to the old, repressive, Apollonian ego in order to gain a transcendent identity. There is the fear of violating the wisdom we have found necessary for coping with life. After all, the reality principle has kept us from walking out third-story windows under the impression that we can fly to the ground!

The Dionysian consciousness advocated by Norman Brown and experienced under psychedelics must be rejected as *the* model for authentic life. The difficulty becomes obvious in the inability of

Brown to make clear the distinction between garden variety schizophrenia and the Dionysian consciousness. When the ego is lost, and with it all sense of the distinction between I and Thou, inside and outside, dream and reality, the self is cut adrift in a world of infinite possibility which is equivalent to insanity.

If the Dionysian consciousness means the loss of rootedness in time and situation, it cuts man off from that tragic limitation which is the source of his need for decision, responsibility, and community; it seduces man into overlooking the something he can become by promising that he can be everything. And as we have seen, this quest after omnipotence is at the root of neurosis and of psychosis. As Ulysses knew when he rejected Calypso's offer of immortality, the price of seeking to live with the gods is giving up the idea of homecoming. The schizophrenic is close to the truth, because he knows the wonder and the horror that exist in the endless wilderness of fantasy and imagination; he knows that there are vistas open to the human spirit that common sense never dreams possible. But he has forgotten how to find his way home, and the wilderness of possibility becomes a place of terror when the self has no location and vocation which define the unique space, time, and community to which it belongs. Dionysus becomes the god of destruction and insanity if he keeps his worshipers in the wilderness with the promise of endless ecstasy rather than sending them back to the quotidian with a renewed vision of what might be possible if the community of man gave up warfare and began dancing together. We must listen to madness to find the seed of wisdom it contains, but we must not make madness an ideal.

Results of Dionysian Pathology

The Dionysian style of consciousness and life becomes pathological at the point where the vision of possibilities makes no place for the limitations which are currently the defining necessity of the human community. Whether this intoxicating vision is elaborated in the language of psychology, politics, or philosophy, the result is the creation of a world view in which chaos destroys cosmos. The world becomes a nexus of happenings which are totally contingent. Chance is king. In schizophrenia, in the psychedelic experience, and in the extremes of Dionysian intoxication, the same illusion rules which governs the world of Antoine Roquentin, the existentialist hero: "Anything can happen." No reason, law, or necessity sets limits to what is possible. The fact that the sun rises daily, that apple trees regularly observe the patterns that govern apple trees, or that human beings cannot fly, is only a matter of chance which may change at any moment. One thing happens after another, but without reason.

When the world is reduced to happenings, all sense of certainty and security is undercut, and anxiety becomes pervasive; if the possibility of novelty becomes total, we experience the world as *tremendum* but not as *fascinans*—as terrifying but not as promising. Thus, the fullness of wonder is destroyed as admiration, for what is given is replaced by anxiety and dread of what may happen. In the theater of the absurd we see what happens when the ontological shock takes place only relative to the horror and absurdity of the world. Sartre also has captured the terror and diffuse anxiety that result from the vision of a totally contingent world. Antoine Roquentin says,

A real panic took hold of me. I didn't know where I was going. I ran along the docks, turned into the deserted streets in the Beuavoisis district; the houses watched my flight with their mournful eyes. I repeated with anguish: Where shall I go? Where shall I go? *Anything* can happen. Sometimes, my heart pounding, I made a sudden right-about-turn: what was happening behind my back? Maybe it would start behind me and when I would turn around, suddenly, it would be too late. As long as I could stare at things nothing would happen.[27]

This terror is similar to the moment in the psychedelic experience when the ecstasy of ego-transcendence has begun to subside and yet the voyager has no control over his consciousness, and the fear arises that his mind will never get back into his body and that he may be condemned to wander forever in the endless possibilities of fantasy. It must also resemble the acute panic which often accompanies the schizophrenic state. Dreams, visions, and fantasy are all sources of nourishment only so long as they do not exile us from the domesticated world of the quotidian which is the headquarters for the human adventure into the unknown of novelty and possibility.

The Dionysian ideal of perpetual spontaneity, of the completely

open and fluid personality and society, or of the careless dance in
the midst of chaos may as easily destroy freedom as the Apollonian
insistence upon law, order, and observing the limits. To advocate
"permanent revolution, and no permanent structures issuing from
contract, commitment, promise, will or will power . . . ."[28] is to
ignore the tragic limits of human existence. De-cision, self-limitation, and choosing a definite style of life are necessary to human
freedom, because neither energy, nor opportunity, nor time is given
to any person to realize all of the theoretical (that is, wonder-ful)
possibilities he bears. To be free is to choose the relationships, institutions, beliefs, and values by which one will be limited and
defined. In his study of fidelity Marcel has shown that significant
freedom resides in the ability to make and keep promises. Where
pure spontaneity is the rule of life, one becomes a slave to the in-
stant and to impulse (as in what Kierkegaard called "the aesthetic
stage of life"). Conversely, the ability to bind ourselves over a
period of time by contracts, promises, and vows is the source of
that continuity which is essential to a sense of selfhood. The foundation of the individual's certainty that he is a unique, potent agent
is nothing other than the sum of promises which have been made
and kept, both *to* the individual and *by* the individual. We were
nurtured and given existence by the web of concern and commitment which was early woven around us by parents and friends,
and we continue to give birth to ourselves only to the degree that
we have the courage to define and limit ourselves by the making
and keeping of promises. In neurosis, psychedelic experience, and
the Dionysian consciousness, the infinite, wonderful possibilities
which are revealed in dreams and fantasy seduce us into the illusion
that there may be authentic existence without de-cision or tragedy.
Such an existence belongs to the gods, and the man who seeks it
loses the feel of the earth upon which he stands.

3. WONDER AND THE AUTHENTIC LIFE— *HOMO TEMPESTIVUS*   •

We are now in a position to gather up many suggestions and
clues and answer the question with which this chapter began: What
is the place of wonder within the economy of the authentic life? By

constructing a broad typology of pathology we have been led to the conclusion that the delicate balance of human existence may be upset by either too little or too much wonder. If the Apollonian personality minimizes wonder in the tightly controlled world it has domesticated by the imposition of philosophical, psychological, or social necessity, the Dionysian personality is inundated by the mysterious givenness of things and is awash in the endless possibilities of the oceanic consciousness.

While we are able to agree with the advocates of the Dionysian consciousness that the dominant personality type in contemporary Western society is repressively Apollonian, and our culture stands in danger of losing the virtues of enthusiasm, hope, spontaneity, celebration, and wonder, we cannot believe that the death of Apollo will lead to their recovery. The apocalyptic demands of the advocates of Dionysus neglect the reality of the psychological and political present by refusing to take responsibility for articulating any appropriate means for moving step by step to freer personality and social structures. They do not speak to the problem of creating a personality structure and social order within which it might become possible to carry on the day-to-day responsibilities of making a living, raising children, and creating a community in a more spontaneous and graceful manner. Away with all permanent structures! Down with the ego and repression! Freedom now! Tune in, turn on, and drop out! While such slogans intoxicate the young and set them to dancing for a time, they tell nothing of the triumph and quiet ecstasy that result from seeing the pursuit of justice prepare the ground for the advent of love, the discipline of five-finger exercises yielding to the creative moment, or patient and courageous decisions resulting in sustained *growth* toward mature freedom. It was wisdom that led the Greek spirit to require the temple at Delphi to be shared by Apollo and Dionysus. Either god worshiped alone leads to madness.

HEALTH AS BALANCE: WONDER AND ACTION

As a guiding star to that balance which is the essence of both sanity and authentic life, we may adopt as a maxim Chesterton's statement, with which this chapter was prefaced. These twin demands of the human spirit for wilderness and home, wonder and welcome, adventure and security, or Dionysus and Apollo may be considered structural principles of the authentic life, as they are also the essential components of all rationality. In defining what he calls "the sentiment of rationality," William James maintains that the philosophic attitude consists of a balance between two cravings. There is, first, the passion for distinguishing—for being acquainted with the particulars, in all their chaotic multiplicity. And second, there is the passion for simplification—for unification of diverse particulars under one universal law. A philosophy which listens only to heterogeneous particulars—which remains in wonder before the givenness of things—fails to get us out of the "empirical sand-heap world"; it leaves us with utter pluralism, which is the psychological equivalent of schizophrenia and the philosophical equivalent of nihilism. Likewise, a philosophy which forces all particulars into an abstract explanatory synthesis, and thus eliminates multiplicity, makes of the world a monotonous plenum in which there is no room for novelty or surprise. An adequate philosophy must preserve the adventure of standing in wonder before the mystery of the given as well as the security of explanations, boundaries, and limits which domesticate chaos.

If authentic life is defined as requiring a balance of Dionysian and Apollonian elements, we may conclude that neither *homo admirans* nor *homo faber* is an adequate model of man. *Homo admirans* accepted the world as a gift and affirmed that the highest and most appropriate human act was contemplation and celebration; however, he refused to assume full responsibility for remaking the world closer to the heart's desire. Poverty, suffering, and the wanton ravages of flood, erosion, and disease have too often been accepted by traditional cultures of East and West as unalterable aspects of the givenness of life with which it is impious to tamper. *Homo faber* has abandoned the notion of the impious and has assumed total responsibility for molding the chaos of nature into the secular city, but in so doing has lost the ability to celebrate anything other than the products of his own hands. The wilderness is not the source of gift for *homo faber;* it is only chaos waiting to be fabricated into something of meaning. Thus he fears all areas in which wildness and spontaneity reign—the dream, the dance, the moment of wonder. If traditional man evaded his responsibility by devoting himself too largely to the Dionysian enthusiasm, modern man has exalted his power to discipline the world to such an extent that he fears and suspects anything grace-ful or gratuitous.

We are in need of a new model of man which will allow us to preserve the valid insights of both traditional and modern, Dionysian and Apollonian, models of man. An adequate model must make clear that what have often been taken as mutually exclusive models of man are more properly seen as different moments in perception and action which must achieve a balance for vivid, full human life to be sustained. In summary, the elements that must be components of an adequate model of man may be represented schematically as those belonging to what we may call the principles of wonder and action.

Wonder

The Dionysian mode of being in the world.

Man-the-dancer responds to experience as it is given in its multiplicity. *Homo ludens* is oriented toward play, levity, fantasy, spontaneity; he is libidinal, erotic, living primarily in feeling and sensation, destroying boundaries and exploring diversity.

Without wonder there is no knowledge of the *world*. Thus, one axis of knowledge is: intuition, silence, welcoming receptivity, relaxation in the presence of the other. In wonder man attends to the kaleidoscopic plurality of the world; he juxtaposes and savors particulars. Wondering knowledge is immediate, sensuous, enthusiastic, a matter of participation and union, an overcoming of the estrangement between subject and object.

Action

The Apollonian mode of being in the world.

Man-the-maker fabricates an environment from the raw material of nature. *Homo faber* is oriented toward work, seriousness, realism, regularity; he is governed by a strong ego, living primarily by thinking and willing, by erecting boundaries, giving form, intellectual and material possession.

Without action there is no *knowledge* of the world. Thus, one axis of knowledge is: judgment, abstraction, categorization, synthesis. Laboring reason goes beyond immediacy in a search for understanding. Intelligence acting upon the world to reduce the chaos of plurality to terms that are manageable. Laboring reason searches for coherence, simplicity, unity, and usefulness. The knowledge which results from laboring reason is pragmatic, objective, universal, and verifiable.

In wonder, value and meaning are discovered as given in the encounter. Authentic life involves the "feminine" moment of opening to, welcoming, nurturing the meanings which are given in the immediacy of sensation, relationship, environment, personality; it involves letting things happen, listening in silence for the meaning that is prior to the word.

In acting, man creates values and meanings by his vows, covenants, contracts, projects. Authentic life involves the "masculine" moment of aggressive control, of projecting and realizing a world; it involves making things happen, speaking the words that shape the world.

Personality begins with the gift of relationship. In the beginning is the breast, the world of total succor. The world of primal experience is a matrix of gift and limitation.

Identity begins with decision and action. To separate the self from the matrix one must pass from what is imposed to what is chosen. In the world of mature experience chosen and given limits are in harmony.

Appropriate responses to the world as given in wonder are: admiration, gratitude, appreciation, celebration, contemplation.

Appropriate responses to the world which must be created by human action are: problematic questioning, searching for explanations, solutions, causes.

This mode of perception and being in the world has traditionally been championed by religion and the arts.

This mode of perception and being in the world has become dominant in the West with the development of secular science and technology.

A philosophical definition of health, creative life, or authentic selfhood must incorporate the dominant emphases of these two modes of being in the world and their respective models of man. The philosopher must resist the ideological demands of religious and secular orthodoxies which create pressure toward the adoption of a model of man which requires the rejection of the insights of all competing models. Health is to be found in balance, in wholeness —in polychrome existence. Orthodoxy always demands purity of heart and foolish consistency. Thus, medieval Christendom created an atmosphere in which it was difficult for the individual to credit his longings for and experience of potency to recreate the world through investigation and action. And in a parallel manner, secular technocracy creates a spiritual climate within which investigation and action are approved, but wonder, hope, and basic trust are suspect. The repressive demand that forces us to choose between wonder or action, grace or responsibility, and gratitude for the gift of life or radical freedom in a contingent world leads to the destruction of the synthesis which is the essence of creative personality. The task of philosophy is to see life steadily and whole; therefore it has the prophetic responsibility of protesting against any ideological castration of man.

THE PRINCIPLE OF OSCILLATION

There is increasing evidence that healthy personality is structured upon a principle of oscillation. Studies reveal that creativity arises out of the interplay between primary and secondary process-thinking (id and ego). The creative process is an oscillation between play and work, fantasy and realism, and imagination and conceptualization. Also, as we saw in dealing with wonder and the growth of reason in children, there is a rhythm in the development of a healthy child between juxtaposing and syncretism, or between incorporating the concrete new items that are given in raw experience and the creation of an overall schema of understanding and explanation. This same process characterizes the ideal harmony of creative adult life. Creative perception and creative action go hand in hand; sensitive perception of concrete particulars is bound up with the creation of wider and more meaningful patterns of explanation and relationship. It is an illusion to believe that we can have one of these modes of relating to the world without the other. Pathology involves just such an effort to deny wonder-openness-novelty-possibility or action-decision-regularity-necessity. Health lies in the both/and (not the either/or): in granting proper reverence to both Dionysus and Apollo. In the mature personality the pendulum is constantly swinging between wonder and action, and the further it swings in one direction, the further it may go in the opposite direction. The more the self is at home in the world it has created by accepting and defining its gifts and limits, the freer it is to wander and appreciate strangeness. Ontological security and ontological wonder increase proportionately. It is the insecure self that lives in anxiety and defensiveness, protecting itself from the intrusion of any novelty which threatens its tenuous integration.

Having the security of a home is the source of the psychological strength necessary to undertake an adventure. In the creative personality the lion and the lamb lie down together without ceasing to be lion and lamb; the gypsy and the homesteader live side by side in peace.

Wisdom as Timeliness

The question naturally arises: How is it possible to combine the virtues of Dionysus and Apollo within a single model of man? By way of answering this we must point out that *both Dionysian and Apollonian models of man are governed by spatial metaphors.* The Dionysian way advises that we break down the *boundaries.* The Apollonian way insists that we observe the *limits* of the possible as they have been set forth by metaphysical vision, social convention, or religious tradition. There is, in the history of philosophy, another organizing principle which cannot be neglected. The wisdom tradition maintains that *time* rather than *space* is the organizing principle for the authentic life. The unity of the authentic life is plural; its wisdom lies in understanding the necessity for the changing moments and seasons of life.

> For everything there is a season, and a time for every matter
>   under heaven:
> a time to be born, and a time to die;
> a time to plant, and a time to pluck up what is planted;
> a time to kill, and a time to heal;
> a time to break down, and a time to build up;
> a time to weep, and a time to laugh;
> a time to mourn, and a time to dance;
> a time to cast away stones, and a time to gather stones together;
> a time to embrace, and a time to refrain from embracing;
> a time to seek, and a time to lose;
> a time to keep, and a time to cast away;
> a time to rend, and a time to sew;
> a time to keep silence, and a time to speak;
> a time to love, and a time to hate;
> a time for war, and a time for peace.[29]

Wisdom comes, usually with age, when a man can look back over his years and realize that there is an economy to the seasons of life. He sees that the times of strife, suffering, and waiting which seemed so difficult to endure were as necessary to the formation of personality as the times of love, joy, and ecstasy. To love and accept the self as it is, is to accept all the moments that formed it.

The difference between the wise man and the fool lies in the sense of timing. *The wise man knows what time it is in his own life and in the life of the community.* He knows that sensing the *kairos* (the prepared or ripe moment) is more important than conforming to the compulsive rhythm of chronological time. Thus, the wise man is able to give himself gracefully to seemingly contradictory experiences, because he knows that they belong to different seasons of life, all of which are necessary to the whole. Spring and winter, growth and decay, creativity and fallowness, health and sickness, power and impotence, and life and death all belong within the economy of being. The fool distrusts the polychrome character of life and hence is always trying to hold on to what is past or to grasp prematurely what is coming. Because of his basic distrust and resentment of the economy of the seasons, the fool loses even the ability to move gracefully within the present. Folly is founded on the conviction that time bears us only toward death and gradually destroys all that is of value to the individual, and therefore it must be resisted. The life of the fool, then, becomes the vain effort to run from death by using the energies of life to create a monument or a memory. Being unable to accept the gracefulness of time, the fool seeks to stem its flow.

THE TIMELY MAN—HOMO TEMPESTIVUS

For the sake of convenience we may christen the model of man recommended by the wisdom tradition in philosophy with the title, *homo tempestivus*—the timely or opportune man, the man for all seasons. In using this designation, we must be careful to guard against the negative connotations which have become associated with opportunism. The opportunist is reckoned to have no integrity or moral purposiveness, hence in any moment—like a chameleon —he changes his moral coloration to blend in with the background in order to serve his own selfish interests. The word "opportune," however, may easily bear the connotation of a strong, but flexible, moral stance. Webster defines opportune as "1. right for the purpose; fitting in regard to circumstances; said of time. 2. happening or done at the right time; seasonable; well timed; timely." Thus, *homo tempestivus* is a proper designation for the man whose wisdom consists of knowing what time (*kairos*) it is. The opportunist belongs to what Kierkegaard called the "aesthetic" mode of existence in which the self, being empty of moral decisiveness and purpose, must be filled from without by the happenings of the moment. The opportune man, on the other hand, has a strong ethical commitment and an equally strong sense of the ambiguities of the situation within which his ethical commitment must be lived out. Given both the wondering sensitivity to the situation and the impulse toward ethical activity and responsibility, *homo tempestivus* seeks to act *appropriately*. Indeed, we may say that the prime ethical ideal of the wise man is appropriate response.

It is, in principle, impossible to create a casuistry of appropriate responses. Perhaps the best metaphor to illuminate the ethical style of *homo tempestivus* is that of the dance. The wise man is a dancer; he hears the music issuing from his situation, he is sensitive to his partners, and he moves boldly to commit himself to the rhythmic patterns that emerge in the dance. The fool always wants the certainty of knowing all the steps before he will commit himself to the dance; thus he is too timid to learn to trust himself to be appropriately moved by the music and the motion. The sense of timing which is the essence of wisdom comes only when one trusts oneself to the dance. One of the great moments in modern literature is when the repressed Apollonian character of "the boss" in Kazantzakis's novel turns to the Dionysian Zorba and says, "Zorba —teach me to dance," for he has then realized that the touch of madness necessary to authentic life is identical with the decision to trust the self to move gracefully when there is no rule of casuistry.

Homo tempestivus avoids the extremes that lead to the Apollonian and Dionysian pathologies without sacrificing the virtues of either god. He is sufficiently endowed with a sense of wonder to refuse to make any premature closure of the limits of the possible. In wondering he finds hope, because he recognizes that to be exiled within the limiting structures of temporal existence is to be ignorant about the range of ultimate possibilities. Because the future is open, he can throw the full weight of his freedom behind the project to which he commits himself, knowing it is impossible to determine in advance the range of novelty that is possible. On the other hand, *homo tempestivus* is sufficiently Apollonian to be aware of the provisional limits which are currently the defining structures of human personality, culture, and historical existence. There is a time to die, and this means that all human existence is under the necessity of defining its limits within the known horizons of the penultimate. There may be ground for the wise man to hope, since the ultimate context of human existence is unknown and unknowable, but the penultimate necessity of death demands a radical decisiveness and resignation to limited possibilities. Both the timeless imagination of the id and the tragic realism of the ego are necessary—both dreams and decisions, wonder and action.

When I was a boy I used to swim in the Indian River Inlet in southern Delaware. Where the outgoing water from the bay met the incoming surge from the ocean, the currents were swift and the waves wild and irregular. Many people lost their lives in these waters, and the inlet was rightly considered extremely treacherous. With a confidence born of folly, I played with the irresistible danger. However, having survived the folly of repeated swimming in dangerous tides, I can now see that I learned something of the principles (if not the practice) of wisdom in those waters. The outgoing currents were too swift to swim against, but if you would only yield yourself to them they would carry you to a point beyond the inlet, where it was possible to swim cross-current and come back to shore in the calm waters in the lee of the jetty that formed the south boundary of the inlet. When swimming in turbulent waters, wisdom lies in knowing when to relax and when to struggle.

The sense of wonder,
that is our sixth sense.
And it is the natural religious sense.
—D. H. LAWRENCE[1]

CHAPTER VII

Wonder, Grace, and Gratitude

(A QUASI-THEOLOGICAL POSTSCRIPT)

1. THE ARCHAEOLOGY OF GRACE: TRUST AND FAITH

I have described the mature man as one who is able to accept the various seasons of experience without the loss of balance. Like an athlete or a dancer, he moves among the ambiguities and limitations of existence with a gracefulness that appears to the spectator effortless and spontaneous. His style of life is marked by simplicity and naturalness. Inevitably graceful action, whether it be that of a gymnast performing on the parallel bars or a patient coming to a creative acceptance of his illness, elicits the response, "He makes it look so easy, even I could do it." Only upon reflection do the complexity and difficulty of grace become obvious. Once I actually attempt to balance on the parallel bars or am forced to struggle with the rising anxiety created by disease, the mystery of grace deepens.

Grace appears so simple it should be common, so natural it should be normal. Yet, in fact, it represents a triumph over awkwardness and dis-ease which is so rare that its occurrence is always something of a miracle. In spite of occasional examples of graceful action, human existence remains, for the most part, awkward and disharmonious. Man is divided against himself: mind against body, ego against id, essence against existence, spirit against flesh, civil

201

virtues against private inclinations, future expectations against past experience, moral obligation against moral inclination, and so on. Gracefulness, maturity, and harmony remain ideals which are seldom exemplified.

The rarity of grace led the Christian tradition to conclude that, whereas man once had the native possibility of graceful existence, it was lost in what can only be described in mythological terms as the fall of man. Historical man is a sinner, and left to his own devices and abilities he is condemned to awkwardness and alienation. He rebels against the conditions of finite existence and thus is unable to achieve that self-acceptance which is the prerequisite of all gracefulness. Only when God intervenes is man saved from estrangement and set free to act gracefully. The Christian tradition has been clear about the supernatural character of grace but unclear about its mechanics and media. It has most often assumed that grace was primarily operative through the sacraments, symbols, and life of the Church. If there was grace outside the Church, it was considered a pale, inadequate reflection of what was more adequately understood and exemplified by the Christian community.

Our approach to grace has been phenomenological rather than theological. I have deliberately chosen diverse examples of what common language would identify as gracefulness in order to suggest that there is a common structure, or essence, of grace which may be identified in both physical and moral action. Description reveals a similarity between the athletic, social, and theological meanings of grace which cannot be overlooked. Unless we are content either to rule out any religious concept of grace or to limit the theological usage of grace to some supernatural transaction which need have no empirically demonstrable results (as in the traditional objective theories of the atonement), we are forced to ask the question about the foundations of grace. Can we assume a common element in all instances of graceful action?

This question raises in turn the questions of the relation between wonder and the holy, philosophical inquiry and religious language, and maturity and piety. A series of questions may help us to focus our inquiry:

Is it the case, as Christian theologians have maintained, that gracefulness must be thought of as a special gift of God?

Is gracefulness a natural, native possibility of the human spirit which may be actualized with no overt reference to theological convictions or institutions?

Can we speak of grace without speaking of God?

Does the search for wisdom lead to the affirmation of God as the source of the courage necessary for accepting the tragic limitations of finite existence?

Is authentic, mature life possible without a religious dimension?

Is there perhaps a cryptoreligious affirmation implicit in the graceful acceptance of the seasons of life, whether or not God-language is spoken?

Is the way of *homo tempestivus* merely an ethic or is it also a way of salvation?

To get at the area of concern suggested by these questions we must examine the archaeology of grace. Archaeology, in this metaphorical sense, deals with the principles, presuppositions, roots, or foundations which underlie a phenomenon. Our inquiry will settle on one question: What kinds of basic attitudes and implicit affirmations must we assume to be present whenever we encounter graceful action? Once we have isolated the attitudinal and affective principle underlying gracefulness, we may then compare the religious and nonreligious expressions of the awareness of this foundation.

The foundations of gracefulness are: *trust* in the context within which action must take place and *confidence* in the ability of the self to undertake appropriate action. Grace involves a casual rather than aggressive stance, a nonthreatened acceptance of the self and the world. In the deepest sense, relaxation is possible only when the context within which action must take place is perceived as friendly to the actor. Indeed, we might describe graceful action as at once relaxed and vigorous. In a context in which relaxed and integrated action is possible, one does not need to be on continual guard against possible danger. But where the context is perceived as hostile, the inner effect is one of tightening and preparing oneself to confront whatever danger threatens. Tension, fear, and anxiety are the results of a vote of "no confidence." By contrast, gracefulness is a manifestation of the working assumption (conscious or unconscious) of the trustworthiness of the self and its context.

Erik Erikson has described basic trust as a necessary component of healthy personality. The earliest modality of trust is mediated to the child by the mother in the experience of nursing. This paradigm experience of the infant with the mother must be recapitulated at a higher level at every stage of the life cycle. As soon as the child is ready to leave the security of the home, he must be willing to affirm that the social matrix of his widening world can be depended upon to be responsive to his needs and actions. Thus, he learns to relax and trust himself in hitherto frightening contexts. Orderly and graceful growth takes place only so long as each new stage of life is met with a reaffirmation of trust. Where trust is missing, the world becomes frightening and alien; persons become potential enemies. In such a dangerous atmosphere, suspicion, hostility, and eternal vigilance are the price of a tenuous identity. In its most graphic form, mistrust is manifest in the paranoid vision of the world in which persons, places, and things are all invested with a malevolent power. The paranoid is then forced to develop rituals which ward off the danger of the world or to retreat from it altogether. Expanded to metaphysical dimensions, the paranoid vision becomes gnosticism—the view that the whole world is a demon-filled prison house created by a hostile deity.

It is not difficult to see the continuity between basic trust and the central affirmation that constitutes the religious consciousness. It is the function of religion to nourish and restore the sense of basic trust by affirming in symbolic language that *the ultimate context of life is succoring and trustworthy*. If we look at the mystery of human existence with as few ideological blinders as possible, the most comprehensive, immediate symbol for the human condition might well be: ? (+ − o)?. Each individual's life is a parenthesis which includes mixed experiences of pleasure, pain, and neutrality. Outside the parenthesis—before birth, after death, and beyond the limits of the present temporal imagination—there is the question mark (mystery). The philosophical task each man faces is to take some symbol from within the parenthesis and use it to interpret the mystery. Theology, making use of the rich emotive language of

love, trust, mercy, and grace, affirms that the source out of which
life comes and into which it disappears intends the fulfillment
rather than the frustration of those values we hold to be fundamental for human dignity. The "ground of being" is trustworthy.
Religion places a + at the heart of the mystery: +? (+ − o)
?+. This is the meaning of the basic religious affirmation: God is
love. H. Richard Niebuhr has expressed the radical nature of the
religious affirmation in this way:

> Our primordial interpretation of the radical action by which we are
> is made in faith as trust or distrust. Between these two there seems to
> be no middle term. The inscrutable power by which we are is either
> for us or against us. If it is neutral, heedless of the affirmations or
> denials of the creatures by each other, it is against us, to be distrusted
> as profoundly as if it were actively inimical. For then it has cast us
> into being as aliens, as beings that do not fit. . . .
> When we say that the power by which we are is God, we may
> express our interpretation in trust, for to say "God" is to say "good"
> in our common speech; the word, God, means the affirmer of our
> being, not its denier; "God" means the concern of the ultimate for
> what issues from it, not its heedlessness or its animosity.[2]

For the religious man, God-language functions to affirm that the
ultimate context into which human existence is inserted is trustworthy. Since human life is rendered ultimately meaningful by its
inclusion in a succoring and careful totality, relaxation, gratitude,
and responsible action are the appropriate modalities of authentic
life. In traditional religious language: man is justified by his faith
in the trustworthiness of God; therefore, human life may be
graceful.

For the nonreligious person, trust may redeem the contingent
world of the happening from absolute terror and nausea and render
hope possible. If what merely happens may be anticipated with
basic trust, then the future is open. Trust undercuts the suspicion
that whatever evades the control of *homo faber* must be terrible
and threatening merely because it is uncontrolled. It is trust that
prepares the way to celebrate what happens in those areas of
human experience which are not amenable to the control of will,
reason, or technique. Chaos, trusted, may give birth to a dancing
star (as Nietzsche hinted); resisted and resented, it becomes an

enemy. A nonreligious affirmation of basic trust may root in a positive doctrine of the absurd: reality overflows explanation, and thus it remains mysterious. Since we cannot understand the limits of the possible or control the happenings that form the context of human history, we must remain open to the emergence of radically novel events which may nourish and refresh. The alternative to such trust is the heroic masochism of Sisyphus which revels in alienation and considers despair the badge of human courage and authenticity. A religiously agnostic form of trust is merely the outcome of epistemological humility: we do not know the limits of the possible; therefore, we hope. The happenings that shape our destiny may as easily elicit celebration as rebellion or resignation.

It would appear that the mature man, whether religious or nonreligious, chooses to credit the context that nourishes and creates him as being worthy of trust, and this is the source of the ability to relax and act gracefully The alternative to such an act of faith is resentment, which leads to the view that the world is alien and hostile to the human spirit. And to live in such an alien and hostile world forces an estrangement between man and his environment which is variously manifested as paranoia, schizophrenia, and gnosticism.

2. THE RHETORIC OF GRATITUDE: WORSHIP AND CELEBRATION

Maturity involves both acceptance and gratitude. Each man enters into life wounded, deformed, and graceless: parents injure their children with prejudice, fear, and carelessness; societies cripple minorities by injustice and hatred; nature brings to birth many of her children with defects and abnormalities. A central task each man faces in the formation of an identity is the acceptance of the deformities and limitations which are his destiny. Self-acceptance is the prelude to responsibility and creative change. Before we may be graceful we must accept our gracelessness. Mere acceptance and resignation, however, are not sufficient; gratitude is, finally, necessary to full integration and self-acceptance. Nietzsche remarked that a man must come to love his wounds. A sensitive analysis of the dynamics of human personality reveals that it is impossible to delete those deformities and limitations which we are all tempted to despise without completely altering the person. To accept and love the self is to come, gradually, to love the battles it has had to fight and the wounds it has sustained. Radical self-acceptance and integration require that we accept all that has made us what we are. To be grateful *that* we are involves gratitude for *what* has made us as we are. Thus, gratitude and forgiveness are both essential to wholeness. That resentment which causes us to despise our wounds and our limits is finally directed not at something that is accidental to our being but at our being itself. Gratitude alone allows us the freedom from our wounds and our past which is necessary for autonomous action. Gracefulness requires that, in the end, we become able to say of those events we are tempted to despise and reject: "In enduring them, I have become fuller and more authentic."

To speak of life as a gift which may be fully enjoyed only where gratitude is acknowledged may seem like blind optimism— whistling in the dark. How is it possible to be grateful for life in the kingdom of earth where injustice, suffering, and tragedy exercise dominion? The problem of evil cannot be ignored if we are to speak realistically about gratitude. Only the insensitive or the ideologist could claim that the conditions of fullness which make gratitude easy are the heritage of every man. For while we all enter into life maimed, some are forced to bear inordinate burdens of pain, injustice, and loneliness. How, then, can we say that gratitude is necessary for the fullness of life?

We must begin by acknowledging the inevitability of failure. There is no hope that we can eradicate evil and tragedy—only that we can find ways of keeping the spirit alive. This being the case, we must be able to speak of gratitude at the same time that we acknowledge the existence of evil. In fact, it is only when we set as a *norm* a model of life in which gratitude is appropriate that we have a standard by which to judge the measure of evil that man creates and suffers. We may judge as a violation of the sanctity of life all that makes gratitude and wonder more difficult or impossible. It is because we define gratitude as a condition of authentic life that we can resist all those concrete forms of injustice and evil that lead inevitably to bitterness and resentment. The tragedies of

Auschwitz, Watts, and Vietnam have the stink of sacrilege precisely because they violate the hope and expectation each human being harbors that his life may achieve its potential fullness. Every man covets the opportunity to take the measure of his life and be able to pronounce the judgment, "It is good." And it is only to the degree that we are able to forge the diverse moments of pain and pleasure, emptiness and fullness, loneliness and love, and failure and success into some meaningful and gracious whole that we are able to escape that resentment and bitterness which form the roots of gnosticism, neurosis, and despair. Finally, the most significant index we have of the stature of a man is the amount of pain and tragedy he has been able to bear and still rejoice in the gift of life. We cannot make unambiguous life the condition of gratitude; if we did, rejoicing and celebration could only be carried on where we ignore the tragic character of actual existence or be postponed until we reach Utopia or Apocalypse. We may (and, indeed, must) speak of the necessity for gratitude without being blind to all that conspires to deny each man his birthright of the possibility of graceful existence.

The traditional religious mode of expressing gratitude is worship. As we have seen earlier, the religious consciousness is constituted by the movement of thought from the given to the Giver, from the contingent to the source, or from the world to God. Worship expresses this movement by focusing upon certain realities which are perceived as symbolic or sacramental. In sacramental objects, persons, words, or places, God—or the holy—is experienced as present in the ordinary. In the sacrament the distance between the quotidian and the sacred is momentarily overcome; the beyond incarnates itself in the everyday. The authentic function of such a symbolic incarnation is to remind the believer that any part of reality may be charged with the grandeur of God. Bread and wine are set apart and consecrated to remind us that all bread and wine—all eating, all being—are dependent upon the gracious and trustworthy power of God. In the act of acknowledging unconditional dependence upon the source of the gift of life and of expressing gratitude for this gift, the sacramental reality set apart in worship becomes a medium of transcendence.

However meaningful worship has been in the past as a means

of expressing gratitude, it is no longer viable for a large (if not major) portion of contemporary society. We have undergone a change in perception. The world is increasingly experienced by modern man as a contingent gift which can be neither explained nor transcended. For those who still find the movement from the given to the Giver viable, worship remains an authentic mode of expressing gratitude. But for those who do not, a new rhetoric of gratitude must be developed. Henry Bugbee has stated the issue well:

The question is whether we can rejoice with things, or whether we find them simply inane. Sartre finds them inane, absurd. Even this would be all right if he rejoiced with them in their absurdity, as Camus rejoices at the close of *The Stranger*. One can celebrate a world in which things "just happen" as does Chekov, and in so doing he may open himself to the understanding of reality as mystery.[3]

There is a distinction between worship and celebration which may help us discover a rhetoric of gratitude which is appropriate for the man whose piety consists of remaining close to the earth. While this distinction is slight and difficult to render precise, it reflects two diverse ways of being in the world. If worship moves from symbol to a transcendent source, *celebration consists of rejoicing in the presence of things* rather than going beyond them. Worship seeks to transcend the object which is its medium, while celebration seeks to penetrate to its depths. Since worship is focused upon events or things that are symbolic of a transcendent realm of meaning, it remains possible only where there is a distinction (if not a dualism) between the sacred and the profane, the sacramental and quotidian, the miraculous and the ordinary, or the supernatural and the natural. Celebration presupposes the dissolving of such distinctions and dualism. We might say that celebration takes place in the one-story, undifferentiated, contingent world where all things merely happen and may not be explained—the world increasingly inhabited by what we like to call "modern man."

It is easier to illustrate than to define the act of celebration which may replace worship as the rhetoric of gratitude for modern man. The movement of the modern mind has been away from explanation to description, away from elaborate ritual and symbolism to simplicity and directness. We might take as a motto to understand the movement of piety which constitutes secular celebration the battle cry that heralded the phenomenological movement in philosophy: "Back to the things themselves!" Philosophy, as well as art, has sought a new immediacy, a new immersion in the primal simplicities of the world which are given in sense and feeling. The search for meaning in the overworld of traditional philosophy and theology has given way to a new and deepened empiricism which remains close to the meanings of the flesh. This change in cognitive style is reflected in the sparse prose of Hemingway or in the bare simplicity of the images of William Carlos Williams. The new search for immediacy also accounts for the growing interest in Zen and the exploration of techniques for awakening sensitivity.

There has been a comparable change in the gravity of the religious consciousness. We may best illustrate this by a passage from one of Van Gogh's letters.

I can very well do without God, both in my life and my painting, but I cannot, ill as I am, do without something which is greater than I, which is my life—the power to create. . . . And in a picture I want to say something comforting as music is comforting, I want to paint men and women with that something of the eternal which the halo used to symbolize, and which we seek to give by the actual radiance and vibration of our colorings.[4]

The holiness which traditional man found in the heights is now sought in the depths. The sacred is incarnate in flesh, things, and events or not at all. The meaning is in the medium; the holiness is homogenized into the quotidian. The light of the eternal is in the vibrancy of the colors; reality is luminous because it is polychrome.

Celebration consists of appreciation, enjoyment, and admiration in the presence of objects, events, and persons that are luminous with meaning, saturated with the potential (promise) of value. It centers in the effort to go to the depth of everyday experience and wonder before the meaning that is given and created in the ambiguous and contingent world in which human consciousness is exiled.

Between the traditional believer and secular man, the worshiper and the celebrant, there is mutual suspicion. The secular man sus-

pects that the language of theology and worship conceals the un-
seemly pride of the effort to transcend the human condition and
therefore falls into ideology or illusion. The modern man who
still finds worship meaningful suspects that the celebration of the
secular man masks an arrogant refusal to render thanks for the
gift of life which can only come from God. We are thus left with
differing answers to the question of which rhetoric of gratitude
is most appropriate—worship or celebration.

The situation may be clarified, if not resolved, by a parable.

When I was six years old I was walking by a courthouse in a
small town in Tennessee. A man came out, followed by a large
crowd. As he walked past me, he pulled a knife from his belt and
said, "I present you with this knife." Before I could see his face
or overcome my shock and thank him, he turned and disappeared.
The knife was a strange and mysterious gift. The handle was made
out of the foot of a deer, and on the blade there was something
written in a foreign language which no one in town could trans-
late. For weeks after this event I lived with a pervasive sense of
gratitude to the stranger and with a wondering expectancy created
by the realization that such a strange and wonderful happening
could occur in the ordinary world of Maryville. If nameless strang-
ers gave such gifts, what surprises might be expected in the world?

The question of the importance of the different languages of
grace and gratitude is analogous to the question: How important is
it to know the name of the stranger and thank him for his gift?
Traditionally, man knew whom to thank for the gift of existence
and created an appropriate language of gratitude. If modern man
is unable to make the leap beyond the gift to name the giver—if
he is unable to read the cipher on the blade of the knife—is he
thereby impoverished?

Our judgment must be that the basic attitudes a person adopts
toward the world are a more significant indication of his psychological and spiritual health than the specific symbols he uses to
express these attitudes. Whether we continue to talk about God
is not so important as whether we retain the sense of wonder which
keeps us aware that ours is a holy place. Whether the language that
gives us our primary orientation to what we consider the ultimate
context of human existence is political, mythological, poetic, philo-

sophical, or theological is not so important as the manner in which the language functions. Any contextual language must be judged by its ability to nurture those attitudes which are essential to authentic life: openness, availability, epistemological humility in the face of the mystery of being, and the ability to admire and be grateful. If we are not to fall into theological, ethical, or political idolatry, we must bear in mind that all symbols, concepts, theories, and myths are inadequate and crude efforts to domesticate a reality that eludes explanation. And if we must live in the anxiety and the splendor of continually reforming the language of our vision and our gratitude, it is well to remember the words of Dag Hammarskjöld: "God does not die on the day when we cease to believe in a personal deity, but we die on the day when our lives cease to be illumined by the steady radiance, renewed daily, of a wonder, the source of which is beyond all reason."[5]

NOTES

PREFACE

[1] W. MacNeile Dixon, *The Human Situation* (New York: Longmans, Green, 1937), p. 429.

CHAPTER I. THE ANATOMY OF WONDER

[1] "Wonder," *N.E.A.* Journal (February, 1957), p. 73.
[2] Ludwig Wittgenstein, *Tractatus Logico-Philosophicus* (London: Routledge & Kegan Paul, 1961), p. 44.
[3] William James, "Sentiment of Rationality," *Will To Believe* (New York: Dover Publications, 1956), p. 72.
[4] Nikos Kazantzakis, *Zorba the Greek* (New York: Simon & Schuster, 1965), p. 152.
[5] *Being and Having* (Westminster, London: Dacre Press, 1949), p. 117.
[6] *Ibid.*, p. 14.
[7] Nikos Kazantzakis, *Report to Greco* (New York: Bantam Books, 1966), p. 430.
[8] Gabriel Marcel, *Metaphysical Journal* (Chicago: Henry Regnery Co., 1952), p. 233.
[9] I. M. Crombie, "Theology and Falsification" in Flew and MacIntyre, eds., *New Essays in Philosophical Theology* (London: S.C.M. Press, 1955), p. 113.
[10] Maurice Merleau-Ponty, *In Praise of Philosophy* (Evanston: Northwestern University Press, 1963), p. 44.
[11] Norman O. Brown, *Life Against Death* (New York: Vintage Books, 1959), p. 245.

CHAPTER II. CHILDHOOD AND WONDER

[1] Quoted in Marshall McLuhan and Quentin Fiore, *The Medium Is the Massage* (New York: Bantam Books, 1967), p. 93.

[2] Norman Cameron, *Personality Development and Psychopathology* (Boston: Houghton Mifflin Co., 1963), p. 36.

[3] Jean Piaget, *Judgment and Reasoning in the Child* (Paterson, N.J.: Littlefield, Adams, & Co., 1964), pp. 246 ff.

[4] *Ibid.*, p. 58.

[5] *Ibid.*, p. 4.

[6] *Ibid.*, p. 61.

[7] *Ibid.*

[8] *Ibid.*, pp. 59–60.

[9] *Ibid.*, p. 61.

[10] G. K. Chesterton, *Orthodoxy* (Garden City, N.Y.: Image Books, 1959), p. 60.

[11] *Op cit.*, p. 233.

[12] Lois Murphy, *The Widening World of Childhood* (New York: Basic Books, 1962), p. 38.

[13] *Ibid.*, p. 192.

[14] A. A. Milne, *Winnie-the-Pooh* (New York: E. P. Dutton & Co., Inc., 1926), p. 11.

CHAPTER III. THE WONDER-FUL COSMOS OF TRADITIONAL MAN

[1] *Patterns of Renewal* (Wallingford, Pa.: Pendle Hill Pamphlet No. 121, undated), p. 9.

[2] "Gnosticism and Modern Nihilism," *Social Research,* XIX (1952), 437.

[3] *Critique of Practical Reason* (New York: Library of Liberal Arts Press, 1956), p. 166.

[4] John Taylor, *The Primal Vision* (Philadelphia: Fortress Press, 1963), p. 72.

[5] Frank Waters, *Book of the Hopi* (New York: Viking Press, 1963), p. 9.

[6] *Ibid.*, p. 191.

[7] *Ibid.*, p. 7.

[8] *Op. cit.*, p. 8.

[9] Bronislaw Malinowski, *Magic, Science, and Religion* (New York: Doubleday & Co., 1954), p. 42.

[10] Mircea Eliade, *The Sacred and the Profane* (New York: Harper & Row, 1961), p. 79.

[11] Plato, *Theaetetus,* 155.

[12] Aristotle, *Metaphysics,* 982b.

[13] *Ibid.*

[14] Aristotle suggested in one place that knowledge would result from the philosophical quest and that intellectual satisfaction would be achieved. He seemed here to equate wonder and curiosity. See *Metaphysics,* 983b.

[15] *The Symposium,* W. Hamilton, trans. (Harmondsworth, Middlesex, Eng.: Penguin Books, 1951), p. 94.

[16] *The Human Condition* (Garden City, N.Y.: Doubleday & Co., 1958), p. 267.

[17] *Ibid.,* p. 16.

[18] Plato, *Timaeus,* 29d.

[19] Walter Kaufmann, ed., *The Portable Nietzsche* (New York: Viking Press, 1954), p. 981.

[20] *Creative Fidelity* (New York: Noonday Press, 1964), p. 22.

[21] Eccles. 1:8.

[22] T. S. Eliot, *Collected Poems* (New York: Harcourt, Brace & World, 1963), p. 4.

CHAPTER IV. THE CHAOTIC WORLD OF MODERN MAN

[1] *The Pensees,* J. M. Cohen, trans. (Baltimore: Penguin Books, 1961), p. 57.

[2] From "A Free Man's Worship," in *Why I Am Not a Christian* (New York: Simon & Schuster, 1957), p. 115.

[3] *Nausea* (New York: New Directions Books, 1959), p. 180.

[4] Max Horkheimer, *Eclipse of Reason* (New York: Oxford University Press, 1947), p. 18.

[5] Sartre, *op. cit.,* pp. 173–76.

[6] "Is American History a Happening?" *Saturday Review of Literature* (March 13, 1967), p. 19.

[7] McLuhan and Fiore, *op. cit.,* p. 53.

[8] Elie Wiesel, *Night* (New York: Pyramid Books, 1961), pp. 76–78.

[9] *Ibid.,* p. 81.

[10] Franklin Baumer, *Religion and the Rise of Skepticism* (New York: Harcourt, Brace & Co., 1960), p. 208.

[11] Eliade, *op. cit.,* p. 203.

[12] Jean Paul Sartre, "Existentialism Is a Humanism," in *Existen-*

tialism, Walter Kaufmann, ed. (New York: Meridian Books, 1956), p. 295.

13 Jonas, *op. cit.,* p. 450.

14 Ernest Hemingway, "A Clean, Well Lit Place," *The Short Stories of Hemingway* (New York: Charles Scribner's Sons, 1938), p. 383.

CHAPTER V. THE TRAVAIL OF HOMO FABER

1 Arendt, *op. cit.,* p. 3.

2 *Man for Himself* (Greenwich, Conn.: Fawcett Premier Books, 1967), p. 53.

3 *Man in Modern Fiction* (New York: Random House, 1949), p. 11.

4 Ayn Rand, *For the New Intellectual* (New York: Signet Books, 1961), p. 130.

5 *Philosophy of Existence* (New York: Philosophical Library, 1949), p. 2.

6 John Steinbeck, *Travels with Charley* (New York: Bantam Books, 1962), p. 31.

7 *Playboy* (January, 1967), pp. 212, 217.

8 *Saturday Review of Literature* (February 5, 1966), p. 27.

9 Ralph Hodgson, *Poems* (London: Macmillan & Co., 1920), p. 70.

10 Augustus Kinzel, "Engineering, Civilization, and Society," *Science* (June 9, 1967), p. 1345.

11 Gerald Sykes, "A New Salvation and a New Supernatural," in *Technology and Human Values,* p. 10.

12 "Industrial Workers' World," *Mass Leisure,* Eric Larrabee, ed. (Glencoe, Ill.: Free Press, 1958), p. 219.

13 David Riesman, "Leisure and Work in Post-Industrial Society," *Mass Leisure,* Eric Larrabee, ed. (Glencoe, Ill.: Free Press, 1958), p. 370.

14 Karen Horney, *Neurosis and Human Growth* (New York: W. W. Norton & Co., 1950), p. 36.

CHAPTER VI. WONDER AND AUTHENTIC LIFE

1 *Orthodoxy* (Garden City, N.Y.: Image Books, 1959), p. 11.

2 The substance of the following two sections will appear in the writer's "Manifesto for a Dionysian Theology," to be published in an academic journal.

3 Friedrich Nietzsche, *The Birth of Tragedy* (New York: Doubleday & Co., 1956), p. 64.

[4] *Ibid.,* p. 24.

[5] *Psychotherapy East and West* (New York: Mentor Books, 1963), p. 60.

[6] Nikos Kazantzakis, *Zorba The Greek* (New York: Simon & Schuster, 1965), p. 300.

[7] C. Landis and F. Mettler, *Varieties of Psychopathological Experience* (New York: Holt, Rinehart, & Winston, 1964), p. 267.

[8] *Ibid.,* p. 263.

[9] *Ibid.,* p. 339.

[10] "The Mechanical Boy," in *Man Alone,* Eric and Mary Josephson, ed. (New York: Dell Publishing Co., 1962), p. 439.

[11] *Ibid.,* p. 442.

[12] Soren Kierkegaard, *Philosophical Fragments* (Princeton, N.J.: Princeton University Press, 1936), p. 66.

[13] Epictetus, *The Encheiridion* in A. I. Melden, *Ethical Theories* (New York: Prentice-Hall, 1955), p. 163.

[14] Gabriel Marcel, *Men Against Humanity* (London: Harvell Press, 1952), p. 116.

[15] Soren Kierkegaard, *Fear and Trembling* and *Sickness unto Death,* in one vol. (Garden City, N.Y.: Doubleday & Co., 1954), p. 173.

[16] Albert Camus *The Myth of Sisyphus* (New York: Random House, 1959), p. 44.

[17] R. D. Laing, *The Divided Self* (London: Penguin Books, 1965), p. 142.

[18] Norman Cameron, *Personality Development and Psychopathology* (Boston: Houghton Mifflin Co., 1963), p. 622.

[19] Landis and Mettler, *op. cit.,* p. 285.

[20] Brown, *op cit.,* p. 151.

[21] *Ibid.,* p. 161.

[22] *Ibid.,* p. 184.

[23] *Ibid.,* p. 262.

[24] *Ibid.,* pp. 159–60.

[25] *Ibid.,* p. 254.

[26] *Ibid.,* p. 235.

[27] Sartre, *op. cit.,* p. 107.

[28] Brown, *loc. cit.*

[29] Eccles. 3:1–8.

CHAPTER VII. WONDER, GRACE, AND GRATITUDE

[1] *The Later D. H. Lawrence* (New York: Alfred A. Knopf, 1959), p. 382.

2 *The Responsible Self* (New York: Harper & Row, 1963), p. 119.

3 *Inward Morning* (New York: Collier Books, 1961), p. 128.

4 Herbert Read, *The Meaning of Art* (London: Faber & Faber, 1951), p. 206.

5 *Markings* (New York: Alfred A. Knopf, 1964), p. 56.

Format by Katharine Sitterly
Set in Linotype Times Roman
Composed, printed and bound by The Haddon Craftsmen, Inc.
HARPER & ROW, PUBLISHERS, INCORPORATED